LEGITIMATION CRISIS

Legitimation Crisis

by JÜRGEN HABERMAS
translated by Thomas McCarthy

BEACON PRESS *Boston*

9 8 7 6 5

Library of Congress Cataloging in Publication Data

Habermas, Jürgen.
    Legitimation crisis.
    Translation of Legitimationsprobleme im Spätkapitalismus.
    Includes index.
    1. Capitalism. 2. Economic history—1945- 3. Social history—20th century.
I. Title.
HC54.H213   301'.045   74-17586
ISBN 0-8070-1520-2
ISBN 0-8070-1521-0 (pbk.)

Contents

Translator's Introduction

Jürgen Habermas is the most influential thinker in Germany today. Picking up where Adorno left off in his exchange with Popper, he became the central figure in the *Positivismusstreit* that dominated German philosophy and sociology in the sixties.[1] Through his detailed criticism of positivist epistemology and methodology and his careful, undogmatic articulation of insights drawn from an immense knowledge of the German philosophical and sociological traditions, he made a lasting contribution to the critical reception of Anglo-American empiricism into German thought. To have brought Kant, Fichte, and Hegel into contact with Wittgenstein, Popper, and Peirce, to have fashioned a language in which Marx, Dilthey, and Freud as well as Dewey, Mead, and Parsons can all have their say, is grounds enough for a claim to intellectual distinction. In recent years, however, Habermas has gone much further in his systematizing efforts. His debate with Gadamer provided a demonstration of the relevance of hermeneutics to social theory.[2] His debate with Luhmann comprises one of the most exhaustive and detailed examinations of the systems-theoretic approach to social inquiry.[3] His formulation of the theory of communicative competence developed the relevance of linguistics and linguistic philosophy to the philosophical foundations of social theory.[4] In short, Habermas has shown himself to be possessed of an astonishing range of interests and competence; and he has succeeded in formulating and developing a unified, systematic perspective in which all this knowledge has its place. Thus, as seasoned an observer of Western intellectual life as George Lichtheim could remark of him in 1969 (that is, *before* the publication of much of his important work):

> The baffling thing about Habermas is that, at an age when most of his colleagues have painfully established control over one corner of the field, he has made himself master of the whole, in depth and breadth alike. There is no corner-cutting, no facile evasion of difficulties or spurious enunciation of conclusions unsupported by research: whether he is refuting Popper, dissecting the pragmatism

of Charles Peirce, delving into the medieval antecedents of Schelling's metaphysics, or bringing Marxist sociology up to date, there is always the same uncanny mastery of the sources, joined to an enviable talent for clarifying intricate logical puzzles. He seems to have been born with a faculty for digesting the toughest kind of material and then refashioning it into orderly wholes. Hegel, whom he resembles at least in his appetite for encyclopaedic knowledge, possessed this capacity in the highest degree, but he was cursed with an abominable style and a perverse fondness for obscurity, whereas Habermas writes as clearly and precisely as any empiricist.[5]

Readers should be forewarned that this last remark is an exaggeration. Habermas can be quite difficult to read, and the present volume is a case in point. It makes unusual demands on the reader, assuming some familiarity with a wide range of disciplines (from economics to ethics), authors (from Kant to Parsons), and approaches (from systems theory to phenomenology). As stated in the author's preface, the intention of the book is a "clarification of very general structures of hypotheses" relating to the dynamics and development of contemporary capitalism. Habermas' aim is no less than that of surveying most of the important literature on advanced capitalist society and organizing it around a continuous line of argument. However, it is extremely important that the reader take Habermas at his word on the status of the argument—it is meant as a *preparatory clarification* of the enormously complex issues involved, preparatory, that is, to the *empirical research* required for their further resolution. The argument makes no claim to finality; certain important questions are left open; and there are numerous indications of the precise points in the argument that call for as-yet-unavailable empirical data. Lest these cautions be taken as a subtle strategy for avoiding criticism, readers should be informed that much of the empirical research in question is already underway at the Max-Planck-Institut zur Erforschung der Lebensbedingungen der wissenschaftlich-technischen Welt.[6]

At its own level, however, that of a dialectical consideration of hypotheses relating to the dynamics of organized capitalism, the argument does make a claim to correctness. To follow the twistings and turnings of this argument, to appreciate the force of points often made in the form of summaries of broad areas of research or in the form of a new direction for an ongoing discussion, requires a great deal of readers. If they are able to meet these demands, they will be appropriately rewarded. Into the great, unformed mass of social and philosophical literature on the character and prospects of contemporary Western society a systematic order is introduced; hypotheses are examined, criticized, revised, and reinterpreted; resolutions of outstanding issues are proposed and unresolved issues stated with admirable clarity with an indication of the information needed to resolve them.

In addition to the general difficulties attendant on the vastness of the literature involved, the intricacy of the line of argument sustained throughout the book, and its tentative, open character at several points, there are three further aspects that may prove troublesome to the Anglo-American reader. First, Habermas examines at some length a variety of theories of economic crisis that have emerged from the Marxist tradition. His discussion, while clear enough in itself, does presuppose some familiarity with the basic ideas of this tradition. This is, perhaps, less of a problem today than in the past. In England and America, there is a growing interest in Marxist economic and political theory. Many of the classic works have been translated, and a number of new studies have recently appeared. For the rest, the reader will find references to the most important literature in the text.

A second—and extremely important—aspect of Habermas' argument is his discussion of systems theory. From his perspective, this includes not only the narrowly cybernetic approaches to society, but functionalist and structural-functionalist approaches as well. His principal targets here are clearly Parsons and Luhmann. Anglo-American readers may be expected to have some acquaintance with the work of the former as well as with the basic categories and methods of socio-cybernetics. The work of Niklas Luhmann, the leading German systems-theorist, is, however, largely unavailable in English. A prolific writer, Luhmann has radicalized the functionalist approach and applied it to a vast number of areas (including law, economics, government, education, and science), concepts (including power, money and influence as well as knowledge and action) and even—reflexively—to systems theory itself. Even though his terminology is often less than transparent, his ideas should have a familiar ring to anyone acquainted with other variants of the systems approach.

Finally, at critical points in his argument Habermas draws on ideas developed in his own theory of communicative competence, with which the average reader can hardly be expected to be familiar. It is this need which I hope partially to fill in the remainder of this introduction. And I shall do so by considering how Habermas' theory responds to two complexes of problems left unresolved by the critical theory of the earlier Frankfurt School.

I. The cleavage between fact and value, description and evaluation, science and criticism, which Hume articulated and the empiricist tradition in philosophy and social inquiry has raised to the status of a first principle, is clearly incompatible with the idea of a critical theory of society. One of the defining characteristics of critical social theory is precisely its attempt to overcome the empirical/normative split and the separation of theory from practice that follows from it. At the level of philosophical foundations, this requires a reconceptualization of the notion of theoretical truth and the establishment of an intimate relation between truth and freedom. Such a reconceptualization was attempted by the earlier Frankfurt School—especially by Max Horkheimer and Herbert Marcuse—in essays published in the *Zeitschrift für Sozialforschung.*[7]

In his *Zeitschrift* essays Horkheimer develops a type of dialectical critique of ideology that refers every thought back to the historical situation in which it arose, to the real context of interests behind it. But critique, says Horkheimer, must be distinguished from scepticism. In making this distinction he appeals to Hegel's concept of concrete negation. In recognizing the dependence and limitedness of any finite truth or isolated perspective, that is, in rejecting its claim to unlimited truth, Hegel does not simply dismiss it out of hand. Instead, he finds for this kind of knowledge—limited, one-sided, isolated—its place in the total system of truth. Thus critique, in the Hegelian sense, does not result in mere negation, in the simple assurance that all determinate knowledge is transitory and worthless, in a word, in a relativism that exhausts itself in the negative enterprise of exhibiting the limitedness—for example, the social and historical context-boundedness—of given theories.

But, of course, Horkheimer cannot simply rely on Hegel to ground the notion of a *materialist* critique. Insofar as the dialectical method in Hegel is part of an idealist system, it must be reconceived.

> In the reflection on his own system Hegel forgets a very definite part of experience. The view that his system is the completion of truth conceals from him the significance of the time-bound interest which influences the individual dialectical presentations as regards the direction of thought, the choice of material and the use of names and words, and which turns his attention from the fact that his conscious and unconscious partiality vis-à-vis the questions of life must necessarily become operative as constitutive elements of his philosophy (PW 242/43).

Thus Horkheimer undertakes to radicalize Hegel's already radically historical approach. (1) He gives up the theologically motivated belief that progress—whatever it might be—is in any way guaranteed. The progress of history depends on the decisions and actions of historical subjects. (2) He distances himself from the conception of a universal history in the strict, that is, Hegelian, sense. Thought, rooted as it is in actual history, can never survey the whole of history as a pre-given totality. Rather it owes its most general categories to the movement of history itself. Finally (3) he accepts the consequences of this context-boundedness for critical theory itself.[8]

The question can then be raised: to what concept of truth, if not to Hegel's, can critical theory appeal in legitimating its own standpoint. Horkheimer describes critical theory as a theory of the contemporary epoch that is guided by an interest in the future, that is, by an interest in the realization of a truly rational society in which men make their own history with will and consciousness. This description gives rise to a related question: in what way can the interest in the future that guides critical theory be distinguished from particularistic interests concealed behind ideological theories? This question obviously must be answered if critical theory itself is to be free from the suspicion of ideology it applies to other theories. How does the conception of freedom on which it relies insure that critical theory too is not just another time-bound (say post-Enlightenment), culture-bound (say secularized bourgeois), and perhaps even "class"-bound (say alienated intellectual) standpoint? I believe a careful reading of the *Zeitschrift* essays will show that Hork-heimer and his colleagues at the Institut für Sozialforschung more or less simply take up the notion of the coincidence of reason and freedom directly or indirectly (that is, through Marx) from Hegel without sufficiently attending to the reworking of philosophical foundations that a rejection of Hegel's idealism entails. For example, when the question arises in "Traditional and Critical Theory," Horkheimer writes: "The viewpoints which critical theory draws from historical analysis as the goals of human activity, especially the idea of a reasonable organization of society that will meet the needs of the whole community, are immanent in human work, but are not correctly grasped by individuals or by the common mind" (p. 213). To anyone familiar with the *Dialectic of Enlightenment* this interpretation of human labor will seem anything but obvious.[9] The point is not which interpretation of work is more correct—work as an anticipation of human freedom or work as introducing essential distortions into man's relationship with nature and with his fellow men (or, to mention another venerable interpretation, work as a necessary evil). The more fundamental question is how does one decide which interpretation is correct and which are ideological distortions.

Another direction taken by Horkheimer (and Marcuse) is to find desire for a rational organization of life and a realization of genuine freedom in the various expressions of culture, in art, religion, and philosophy. But, conversely, these cultural expressions also function in sanctioning the established order of things. This double character of "affirmative culture"—its sanctioning of and protest against existing conditions—requires, therefore, on the part of the critical theorist, an ability to differentiate in his interpretations between regressive and progressive moments.[10] This, according to both Horkheimer and Marcuse, he can do only on the basis of his interest in the future. "A certain concern is also required if these tendencies are to be perceived or expressed" (TCT, p. 213). But now we have moved in a circle, since it was precisely the legitimacy of this interest, its universal and non-ideological character, that we wished to ground.

For the rest, we have numerous suggestive remarks but rather too little philosophical elaboration of how, in a materialist theory of history, the idealist convergence of reason and freedom might be grounded. In one place Horkheimer says: "Thought does not spin such a possibility out of itself but rather becomes aware of its own proper function" (TCT, p. 212). This sounds promising. But what is required, and what is lacking in the *Zeitschrift* essays, is a philosophical elucidation of thought on materialist presuppositions, which, while overcoming Hegel's idealism, does not fall below the level of insight he achieved.

Habermas attempts to accomplish this through a linguistic reformulation of the philosophical foundations of historical materialism. In his discussion of Hegel's Jena *Philosophy of Mind*, in his critique of science and technology as the modern ideology, as well as in *Knowledge and Human Interests*, language is characterized as a universal medium (along with work and domination) in which the social life of the human species unfolds.[11] The socio-cultural form of life is bound to systems of symbolically mediated interaction. Furthermore, recent developments in linguistics and linguistic philosophy have made it clear that "today the problem of language has replaced the traditional problem of consciousness."[12] On the other hand, contemporary analysis as well as idealism and hermeneutics have misconceived the unique structure of communication in ordinary language. An adequate conception can be developed, Habermas argues, only in terms of a universal pragmatics that exhibits the normative basis of all communication *and* explains the possibility of systematically distorted communication. In the next few pages I shall attempt to bring together some of the main ideas of his theory of communicative competence: the relation between communicative action or interaction and discourse, the consensus theory of truth, and the supposition of the ideal speech situation.[13]

According to Habermas, a smoothly functioning language game rests on a background consensus formed from the mutual recognition of at least four different types of validity claims [*Geltungsansprüche*] that are involved in the exchange of speech acts: claims that the utterance is understandable, that its propositional content is true, and that the speaker is sincere in uttering it, and that it is right or appropriate for the speaker to be performing the speech act. In normal interaction, these implicitly raised validity claims are naively accepted. But it is possible for situations to arise in which one or more of them becomes problematic in a fundamental way. In such cases—that is, when the background consensus is fundamentally called into question—specific forms of problem resolution are required to remove the disturbance and restore the original, or a new, background consensus. Different forms are needed for each type of claim. But the validity of problematic truth claims or of problematic norms can be redeemed discursively and only discursively, that is by entering into a discourse whose sole purpose is to judge the truth of the problematic opinion or the correctness of the problematic norm. In the first case we have what Habermas calls a theoretic discourse; in the second, a practical discourse.

The speech situation of discourse represents a break with the normal context of interaction in that, ideally, it requires a "suspension of the constraints of action," a putting out of play of all motives except that of a willingness to come to an understanding, and a "bracketing of validity claims"—that is, a willingness to suspend judgment as to the existence of certain states of affairs (that may or may not exist) and as to the rightness of certain norms (that may or may not be correct). On the other hand, the normal context of interaction does contain an implicit reference to discourse. Insofar as interaction involves regarding the other as subject, it involves supposing that he knows what he is doing and why he is doing it; there is an assumption that he intentionally holds the beliefs he does and intentionally follows the norms he does, and that he is capable of discursively justifying them if the need should arise.

Habermas argues that this supposition of accountability, this expectation that the other could account for his behavior in the same way that (we are convinced) we could account for ours, is a normal feature of functioning language games. At the same time he is well aware that the assumption is usually counterfactual, that the exception is the rule in human history.

We know that institutionalized actions do not as a rule fit this *model of pure communicative action,* although we cannot avoid counterfactually proceeding as if the models were really the case—on this unavoidable fiction rests the humanity of intercourse among men who are still men.[14]

That this assumption is counterfactual and that it nevertheless persists as an expectation can, according to Habermas, he explained in a theory of systematically distorted communication.

> But if this is the case, how can the counterfactual expectations be stabilized? This can be achieved only through legitimation of the ruling systems of norms and through the anchoring of the belief in legitimacy in systematic barriers to will-forming communication. The claim that our norms can be grounded is redeemed through legitimizing world-views. The validity of these world-views is in turn secured in a communication structure that excludes discursive will-formation . . . the barriers to communication which make a fiction precisely of the reciprocal imputation of accountability, support at the same time the belief in legitimacy that sustains the fiction and prevents its being found out. That is the paradoxical achievement of ideologies, whose individual prototype is the neurotic disturbance.[15]

The recognition of the ideality or counterfactual character of the expectation of discursive justifiability for beliefs and norms reflects clearly on the situation of discourse as well. In the light of the possibility of systematic distortion, how can a discursively realized agreement be distinguished from the mere appearance of discursively founded agreement? Which, that is, are the criteria of a "true" as opposed to a "false" consensus? If there are no reliable criteria, then Habermas' recourse to the theory of communication will have left him with many of the same problems as, I have argued, attend earlier versions of critical theory.

In his inaugural lecture of 28 June 1965, at Frankfurt University, Habermas proclaimed that his theory of knowledge and human interests remained faithful to the core of the classical tradition of philosophy, that is, to the "insight that the truth of statements is linked in the last analysis to the intention of the good and true life." [16] His recent work on the consensus theory of truth can be seen as an attempt to make good on this claimed linkage. Once called into question, truth claims can be justified only discursively, through argumentation. "Experiences *support* the truth claim of assertions. . . . But a truth claim can be redeemed only through argumentation. A claim *founded* [*fundiert*] on experience is by no means a *justified* [*begründet*] claim." [17] The elucidation of the notion of truth thus requires an analysis of the discursive justification of validity claims. Discursive justification is a normative concept. Were every contingently conceived agreement to be understood as a "consensus," then the latter obviously could not serve as the criterion of truth. "Truth is not the fact that a consensus is realized, but rather that at all times and in any place, if we enter into a discourse a consensus can be realized under conditions that identify it as a justified consensus. Truth means 'warranted assertability.' " [18] The problem is then, under what conditions is a consensus a justified consensus?

If the criterion that serves to distinguish a true from a false consensus itself requires discursive justification we are moving in a circle; if not, we have transcended the consensus framework in establishing it. The only way out of this dilemma, according to Habermas, leads through a characterization of the "force of the better argument" entirely in terms of "formal properties of discourse"—that is, through an analysis of the notion of "providing rational grounds" [19] in terms of the formal (not in the usual syntactical or semantical senses, but in the pragmatic sense) properties of argumentation.

The very act of participating in a discourse, of attempting discursively to come to an agreement about the truth of a problematic statement or the correctness of a problematic norm, carries with it the supposition that a genuine agreement is possible. If we did not suppose that a justified consensus were possible and could in some way be distinguished from a false consensus, then the very meaning of discourse, indeed of speech, would be called into question. In attempting to come to a "rational" decision about such matters, we must suppose that the outcome of our discussion will be the result simply of the force of the better argument and not of accidental or systematic constraints on discussion. This absence of constraint, this exclusion of systematically distorted communication, Habermas argues, can be characterized formally, that is in terms of the pragmatic structure of communication. His thesis is that the structure is free from constraint only when for all participants there is a symmetrical distribution of chances to select and employ speech acts, when there is an effective equality of chances to assume dialogue roles. In particular, all participants must have the same chance to initiate and perpetuate discourse, to put forward, call into question, and give reasons for or against statements, explanations, interpretations, and justifications. Furthermore, they must have the same chance to express attitudes, feelings, intentions and the like, and to command, to oppose, to permit, and to forbid, etc. These last requirements refer directly to the organization of interaction, since the freeing of discourse from the constraints of action is only possible in the context of pure interaction. In other words, the conditions of the ideal speech situation must insure not only unlimited discussion but also discussion which is free from all constraints of domination, whether their source be conscious strategic behavior or communication barriers secured in ideology and neurosis. Thus, the conditions for ideal discourse are connected with conditions for an ideal form of life; they include linguistic conceptualizations of the traditional ideas of freedom and justice. "Truth," therefore, cannot be analyzed independently of "freedom" and "justice."

It is apparent that the conditions of actual speech are rarely, if ever, those of the ideal speech situation. But this does not of itself make illegitimate the *ideal*—that can be more or less adequately approximated in actual speech situations—which can serve as a guide for the institutionalization of discourse or the critique of systematically distorted communication. If in every discussion we assume that we are really discussing, that we can come to a genuine consensus, and that we are in a position to distinguish a genuine from an illusory consensus; if, furthermore, the ideal speech situation represents those conditions under which a consensus is genuine or rationally motivated; and if, nevertheless, we cannot in any actual discussion empirically determine with certainty whether the conditions of the ideal speech situation do obtain, then:

the ideal speech situation is neither an empirical phenomenon nor simply a construct, but a reciprocal supposition [*Unterstellung*] unavoidable in discourse. This supposition can, but need not be, counterfactual; but even when counterfactual it is a fiction that is operatively effective in communication. I would therefore prefer to speak of an anticipation of an ideal speech situation. . . . This anticipation alone is the warrant that permits us to join to an actually attained consensus the claim of a rational consensus. At the same time it is a critical standard against which every actually realized consensus can be called into question and tested.[20]

Whether this anticipated form of communication, this anticipated form of life, is simply a delusion, or whether the empirical conditions for even its approximate attainment can be practically realized is a question that does not admit of an *a priori* answer. "The fundamental norms of rational speech that are built into universal pragmatics contain, from this point of view, a practical hypothesis." [21]

The theory of communicative competence is a sweeping attempt to reconceptualize the philosophical foundations of the theory-practice problematic. While rejecting a return to the ontological and epistemological views of classical philosophy, Habermas seeks (in opposition to positivism) to reformulate and defend some of its central theses: the inseparability of truth and goodness, of facts and values, of theory and practice. With these theses stands or falls the attempt to provide philosophical foundations for a *critical* theory of society, for a social theory designed with a *practical* intention: the self-emancipation of men from the constraints of unnecessary domination in all its forms. His argument is, simply, that the emancipated form of life that is the goal of critical theory is inherent in the notion of truth: it is anticipated in every act of communication.

II. In the first of his *Theses on Feuerbach*, Marx proclaimed the necessity of going beyond both traditional materialism and idealism:

The chief defect of all previous materialism (including Feuerbach's) is that the object, actuality, sensuousness is conceived only in the form of the *object or perception*, but not as *sensuous human activity, practice*, not subjectively. Hence in opposition to materialism the *active* side was developed by idealism—but only abstractly since idealism naturally does not know actual, sensuous activity as such.[22]

In distinguishing his own, materialistically conceived, form of critique from the philosophical modes of critique developed by Hegel and the Left Hegelians, Marx interprets this "sensuous human activity," this "practice," as labor; material production becomes the basic paradigm for his analysis of human action. Of course, this tendency to reduce *praxis* to *techné*, to instrumental action, is offset somewhat by Marx's conception of labor as *social labor:* the productive activity of man takes place in a symbolically mediated institutional setting; productive forces are applied to nature only within definite relations of production. Nevertheless, material production and social interaction are not viewed as two irreducible dimensions of human practice. Instead, the latter is incorporated into the former. Thus, for Marx, the reproduction of the human species takes place primarily in the dimension of the reproduction of the material conditions of life. In capitalist society, in particular, all social phenomena must ultimately be explained in terms of their material, that is, economic, basis. This reductivist line of thought is clearly expressed in the famous Preface to *A Contribution to the Critique of Political Economy*:

> In the social production of their existence, men inevitably enter into definite relations, which are independent of their will, namely relations of production appropriate to a given stage in the development of their material forces of production. The totality of these relations of production constitutes the economic structure of society, the real foundation, on which arises a legal and political superstructure and to which corresponds definite forms of social consciousness. The mode of production of material life conditions the general process of social, political and intellectual life. It is not the consciousness of men that determines their existence, but their social existence that determines their consciousness.[23]

It is equally clear, however, that Marx's own critique of political economy transcends the narrow categorial framework he articulated. His empirical analyses incorporate in an essential way the institutional framework, the structure of symbolic interaction and the role of cultural tradition. To this dimension belong the configurations of consciousness that Marx calls ideology, as well as their reflective critique—the formation of class consciousness and its expression in revolutionary practice. His theory is essentially a "critical" theory. It is at one and the same time an analysis of the crisis-ridden dynamics of the capitalist economy *and* a critique of ideology, an empirical theory *and* the critical consciousness of revolutionary practice. It becomes practical only by awakening class consciousness through initiating a process of self-understanding. On this reading—which is essentially that of Habermas—there is a basic unresolved tension in Marx between the reductivism of his categorial framework and the dialectical character of his concrete social inquiry.[24]

From the time of the Second International, this ambiguity was resolved in "official" Marxism by an almost exclusive focus on the reductivist, determinist side of Marx's thought. Dialectical materialism became a general ontology of nature, history, and thought, enabling its practitioners to discover their laws of development. The discovery of the laws of motion of society and history would permit prediction and control of social processes. In this form, "DiaMat" could assume the ideological function of legitimating party politics and technocratic social management. Ideology, as a particular case of the general dependence of thought on matter, forfeited the internal relation to critique and revolution that it held for Marx. The critique of political economy, viewed as a deterministic science of the "iron laws" of the development and inevitable downfall of capitalism, could legitimate the sundering of "revolutionary practice" from the formation of class consciousness—in a variety of forms from "vanguard" activism to opportunistic quietism.

While presupposing the essential correctness of Marx's critique of political economy, the early publications of the Frankfurt School already questioned the assumption that the internal development of capitalism would not only create the objective conditions for a classless society, but the subjective conditions for the self-emancipation of the proletariat as well. There was a recognized need to supply the "missing link" between Marx's critique of political economy and his theory of revolution through systematically incorporating the socio-cultural dimension neglected by "mechanical" Marxism. Post-World War I capitalism was no longer liberal capitalism. The growth of the interventionist state, the progressive rationalization and bureaucratization of societal institutions, the increasing interdependence of science and technology, and the "reification" of consciousness were aspects of a new social formation whose analysis required a further development of Marx's thought.

In their major collaborative effort of the post-emigration years, the *Dialectic of Enlightenment*, Horkheimer and Adorno clearly articulated the revision of the categorial framework of historical materialism that had been underway since Lukács. For Marx, natural science was the paradigm of a mode of thinking that constantly proved its truth in practice; it was philosophy that had to be overcome. For Horkheimer and Adorno, it was the contrary: the critique of scientism was the precondition of restoring Marxist theory as critique. Philosophical idealism, in which the ideals of reason and freedom were kept alive—albeit in a distorted form— was replaced by positivistic materialism as the chief enemy of critical thought. The critique of instrumental reason became the fundamental task of critical social theory. For in creating the objective possibility of a truly free society, the progressive mastery of nature through science and technology simultaneously transformed the potential subjects of emancipation. The reification of consciousness was the price paid for the progressive liberation from material necessity. Technocratic consciousness, by eliminating the distinction between the technical and the practical, represented "the repression of ethics as such as a category of life." [25] It could only be overcome, therefore, through a restoration of the dimension of the practical as such. For Horkheimer and Adorno (and Marcuse), human emancipation could be conceived only as a radical break with "instrumental" or "one-dimensional" thought.

In focusing on the process of rationalization and the attendant manifestations of instrumental rationality, they succeeded in restoring the socio-cultural component of dialectical social theory. But, especially in the post-emigration years, this success was accompanied by a marked weakening of the links to the critique of political economy. In the final analysis, the early Frankfurt School did not so much integrate the psychological, social, and cultural dimensions into Marxist political-economic thought as replace the latter with the former. In contrast to the central position that the category of labor occupied in Marx's work, Horkheimer felt that "to make labor a transcendent category of human activity is an ascetic ideology." [26] And Adorno is reported as saying that Marx wanted to turn the whole world into a giant workhouse. [27] What began as a conscious attempt to supplement a previously too exclusive concern with the economic basis by means of analysis of the cultural superstructure ended in a version of pessimistic *Kulturkritik*.

In his reformulation of the basic assumptions of historical materialism, Habermas explicitly introduces a categorial distinction that he feels was implicit in Marx's work: the distinction between labor and interaction. [28] Marx's concept of "sensuous human activity" is analyzed into two components that, while analytically distinguishable and mutually irreducible, are interdependent in actual social practice: instrumental or purposive-rational [*zweckrationale*] action and communicative action or social interaction. Social systems expand their control over outer nature with the help of forces of production. For this they require technically utilizable knowledge incorporating empirical assumptions with a claim to truth. "Inner nature" is adapted to society with the help of normative structures in which needs are interpreted and actions are prohibited, licensed or enjoined. This transpires in the medium of norms that have need of justification. According to Habermas, it is only on the basis of the distinction between work according to technical rules and interaction according to valid norms that we can reconstruct the development of the human species as a historical process of technological and—interdependently—institutional and cultural development. Political emancipation cannot be identified with technical progress. While rationalization in the dimension of instrumental action signifies the growth of productive forces and extension of technological control, rationalization in the dimension of social interaction signifies the extension of communication free from domination.

Habermas develops this distinction at a number of levels. At a "quasi-transcendental" level, the theory of cognitive [*erkenntnisleitenden*] interests distinguishes the technical interest in prediction and control of objectified processes from the practical interest in the maintenance of distortion-free communication. [29] At a methodological level, Habermas argues for a logical distinction among empirical-analytic sciences that aim at technically exploitable nomological knowledge, historical-hermeneutic sciences that aim at the preservation and expansion of a mutual understanding capable of orienting action, and the critical sciences—such as psychoanalysis and critique of ideology—that aim at self-reflective emancipation from systematic distortions of communication.[30] At the sociological level, subsystems of purposive-rational action are distinguished from the institutional framework in which they are embedded.[31] And at the level of social evolution, the growth in productive forces and technological control is distinguished from the extension of communication free from domination.

In drawing these analytic distinctions, Habermas' intention is clearly to overcome the reductivism of Marx's categorial framework without "falling behind" Marx into the kind of left-Hegelianism, unscientific utopianism, pessimistic *Kulturkritik*, and the like, of which the earlier Frankfurt School has been accused. Neither analyses of the economic "basis" nor analyses of the socio-cultural "superstructure" are adequate in themselves to comprehend the dynamics of advanced-capitalist society. The long proclaimed "dialectical" interdependence of the different spheres of society must be reflected at the categorial and methodological levels if critical theory is to avoid the extremes of economism and neo-idealism.

Thus the theory of communicative competence is not intended as an idealist replacement for historical materialism. If it is to provide a satisfactory metatheoretical framework for understanding social evolution it must, in Habermas' view, be "linked convincingly with the precisely rendered fundamental assumptions of historical materialism." [32] This linkage was already initiated in *Knowledge and Human Interests* and further developed in the works that followed. In his debate with Luhmann, for example, Habermas argued at length that an adequate theory of social evolution would have to proceed in three dimensions: the development of the forces of production; the development of organizational forms and techniques that enhance the steering capacity of societies; and the development and critical dissolution of legitimating interpretive systems.[33] In the present work, we are presented with an argument that attempts to integrate the economic, political, and socio-cultural dimensions in a way that earlier critical theorists were convinced was necessary but which they failed to achieve. Whether Habermas has been more successful is for the reader to decide. To the degree that he has, this work constitutes an important contribution to the critical theory of contemporary society.

I should like to thank David Held, Larry Simon, and Jeremy Shapiro for reading the first draft of this translation and offering numerous suggestions; MaryAnn Lash of Beacon Press and Roberta Clark for their editorial support and criticism; Linda Richards for typing the manuscript; Jürgen Habermas for his encouragement and willingness to respond to frequent inquiries; and Nikolaus Lobkowicz for the years at the University of Munich during which my interest in Habermas' work developed.

Thomas McCarthy
Boston University

Preface

The application of the Marxian theory of crisis to the altered reality of "advanced capitalism" leads to difficulties. This fact has given rise to interesting attempts to conceive of old theorems in new ways or, alternatively, to develop new crisis theorems in their place. In the preparatory phase of empirical projects at the Max-Planck-Institute we have also examined such approaches; the argumentation sketched in Part II of my essay sums up what I have learned from these discussions. The departure from custom in referring to in-house working papers[1] is intended to clarify the context in which I am working and, above all, to indicate the unfinished character of the discussions, which have by no means yet led to consensus. In addition, I am concerned that the clarification of very general structures of hypotheses not be confused with empirical results.

The programmatic character of Part I of this book makes clear that a theory of social evolution, although it must be the foundation of social theory, is today still scarcely at all developed. On the other hand, the indeterminate character of Part III shows the close connection between material questions of a theory of contemporary social formation and foundational problems that—as I hope to show soon—can be clarified within the framework of a theory of communicative competence.[2]

J.H.

Starnberg, West Germany
February 1973

PART I

A Social-Scientific Concept of Crisis

Chapter 1. System and Life-World

To use the expression "late capitalism" is to put forward the hypothesis that, even in state-regulated capitalism, social developments involve "contradictions" or crises.[1] I shall therefore begin by elucidating the concept of crisis.

Prior to its employment as a social-scientific term, the concept of crisis was familiar to us from its medical usage. In that context it refers to the phase of an illness in which it is decided whether or not the organism's self-healing powers are sufficient for recovery. The critical process, the illness, appears as something objective. A contagious disease, for example, is contracted through *external* influences on the organism; and the deviations of the affected organism from its goal state [*Sollzustand*]—the normal, healthy state—can be observed and measured with the aid of empirical parameters. The patient's consciousness plays no role in this; how he feels, how he experiences his illness, is at most a symptom of a process that he himself can scarcely influence at all. Nevertheless, we would not speak of a crisis, when it is medically a question of life and death, if it were only a matter of an objective process viewed from the outside, if the patient were not also subjectively involved in this process. The crisis cannot be separated from the viewpoint of the one who is undergoing it—the patient experiences his powerlessness *vis-à-vis* the objectivity of the illness only because he is a subject condemned to passivity and temporarily deprived of the possibility of being a subject in full possession of his powers.

We therefore associate with crises the idea of an objective force that deprives a subject of some part of his normal sovereignty. To conceive of a process as a crisis is tacitly to give it a normative meaning—the resolution of the crisis effects a liberation of the subject caught up in it.

This becomes clearer when we pass from the medical to the

dramaturgical concept of crisis. In classical aesthetics, from Aristotle to Hegel, crisis signifies the turning point in a fateful process that, despite all objectivity, does not simply impose itself from outside and does not remain external to the identity of the persons caught up in it. The contradiction, expressed in the catastrophic culmination of conflict, is inherent in the structure of the action system and in the personality systems of the principal characters. Fate is fulfilled in the revelation of conflicting norms against which the identities of the participants shatter, unless they are able to summon up the strength to win back their freedom by shattering the mythical power of fate through the formation of new identities.

The concept of crisis developed in classical tragedy also has a counterpart in the concept of crisis found in the idea of history as salvation.[2] This figure of thought entered the evolutionary social theories of the nineteenth century through the philosophy of history of the eighteenth century.[3] Thus Marx developed, for the first time, a social-scientific concept of system crisis;[4] it is against this background that we speak today of social or economic crises. When, for instance, we mention the great economic crisis of the early thirties, the Marxian overtones are unmistakable. But I do not wish to add to the history of Marxian dogmatics yet another elucidation of his crisis theory.[5] My aim is rather to introduce systematically a social-scientifically useful concept of crisis.

In the social sciences today a systems-theoretic concept of crisis is frequently used.[6] According to this systems approach, crises arise when the structure of a social system allows fewer possibilities for problem solving than are necessary to the continued existence of the system.[7] In this sense, crises are seen as persistent disturbances of *system integration*. It can be objected against the social-scientific usefulness of this concept that it does not take into account the *internal* causes of a "systematic" overloading of control capacities (or of a "structural" insolubility of control problems). Crises in social systems are not produced through accidental changes in the environment, but through structurally inherent system-imperatives that are incompatible and cannot be hierarchically integrated. Structurally inherent contradictions can, of course, be identified only when we are able to specify structures important for continued existence. Such essential structures must be distinguishable from other system elements, which can change without the system's losing its identity. The difficulty of thus clearly determining the boundaries and persistence of social systems in the language of systems theory raises fundamental doubts about the usefulness of a systems-theoretic concept of social crisis.[8]

For organisms have clear spatial and temporal boundaries; their continued existence is characterized by goal values [*Sollwerte*] that vary only within empirically specifiable tolerances.[9] Social systems, on the contrary, can assert themselves in an hypercomplex environment through altering either system elements or goal values, or both, in order to maintain themselves at a new level of control. But when systems maintain themselves through altering both boundaries and structural continuity [*Bestand*], their identity becomes blurred. The same system modification can be conceived of equally well as a learning process and change or as a dissolution process and collapse of the system. It cannot be unambiguously determined whether a new system has been formed or the old system has merely regenerated itself. Of course, not all systemic alterations in a social system are also crises. The range of tolerance within which the goal values of a social system can vary without critically endangering its continued existence or losing its identity obviously cannot be grasped from the objectivistic viewpoint of systems theory. Systems are not presented as subjects; but, according to the pre-technical usage, *only* subjects can be involved in crises. Thus, only when members of a society experience structural alterations as critical for continued existence and feel their social identity threatened can we speak of crises. Disturbances of system integration endanger continued existence only to the extent that *social integration* is at stake, that is, when the consensual foundations of normative structures are so much impaired that the society becomes anomic. Crisis states assume the form of a disintegration of social institutions.[10]

Social systems too have identities and can lose them; historians are capable of differentiating between revolutionary changes of a state or the downfall of an empire, and mere structural alterations. In doing so, they refer to the interpretations that members of a system use in identifying one another as belonging to the same group, and through this group identity assert their own self-iden-

tity. In historiography, a rupture in tradition, through which the
interpretive systems that guarantee identity lose their social
integrative power, serves as an indicator of the collapse of social
systems. From this perspective, a social system has lost its identity
as soon as later generations no longer recognize themselves within
the once-constitutive tradition. Of course, this idealistic concept of
crisis also has its difficulties. At the very least, a rupture in tradition
is an inexact criterion, since the media of tradition and the forms of
consciousness of historical continuity themselves change historically. Moreover, a contemporary consciousness of crisis often turns
out afterwards to have been misleading. A society does not plunge
into crisis when, and only when, its members so identify the
situation. How could we distinguish such crisis ideologies from valid
experiences of crisis if social crises could be determined only on the
basis of conscious phenomena?

Crisis occurrences owe their objectivity to the fact that they issue
from unresolved steering problems.[11] Identity crises are connected
with steering problems. Although the subjects are not generally
conscious of them, these steering problems create secondary
problems that do affect consciousness in a specific way—precisely
in such a way as to endanger social integration. The question then
is, when do such steering problems arise? A social-scientifically
appropriate crisis concept must grasp the connection between
system integration and social integration. The two expressions
"social integration" and "system integration" derive from different
theoretical traditions. We speak of social integration in relation to
the systems of institutions in which speaking and acting subjects are
socially related [*vergesellschaftet*]. Social systems are seen here as
life-worlds that are symbolically structured.[12] We speak of system
integration with a view to the specific steering performances of a
self-regulated *system*. Social systems are considered here from the
point of view of their capacity to maintain their boundaries and
their continued existence by mastering the complexity of an
inconstant environment. Both paradigms, life-world and system, are
important. The problem is to demonstrate their interconnection.[13]
From the life-world perspective, we thematize the normative
structures (values and institutions) of a society. We analyze events
and states from the point of view of their dependency on functions

of social integration (in Parsons's vocabulary, integration and pattern maintenance), while the non-normative components of the system serve as limiting conditions. From the system perspective, we thematize a society's steering mechanisms and the extension of the scope of contingency.[14] We analyze events and states from the point of view of their dependency on functions of system integration (in Parsons's vocabulary, adaptation and goal-attainment), while the goal values serve as data. If we comprehend a social system as a life-world, then the steering aspect is screened out. If we understand a society as a system, then the fact that social reality consists in the facticity of recognized, often counterfactual, validity claims is not taken into consideration.

To be sure, the conceptual strategy of systems theory encompasses normative structures within its language; but it conceptualizes every social system from the point of view of its control center. Thus in differentiated societies, the political system (as a separate control center) assumes a superordinate position *vis-à-vis* the socio-cultural [15] and economic systems. The following schema is taken from a working paper.[16]

Economic System	Steering Performances ←	Political-Administrative System	Social Welfare Performances →	Socio-Cultural System
	Fiscal Skim-off →		Mass Loyalty ←	

Pre-Political Determinants of the Normative Systems

In the analytic framework of systems theory, social evolution (which takes place in three dimensions: development of productive forces; increase in system autonomy—power; and change in normative structures) is projected onto the single plane of the expansion of power through the reduction of environmental complexity. This projection is seen in Niklas Luhmann's reformulation of fundamental sociological concepts. I have attempted elsewhere[17] to demonstrate that validity claims constitutive for the cultural reproduction of life—such as claims to truth and to correctness/

appropriateness [*Richtigkeit/Amgemessenheit*]—forfeit the sense of discursive redeemability [*Einlösbarkeit*] if they are comprehended as control media and placed on the same level with other media such as power, money, confidence, influence, etc. Systems theory can allow only empirical events and states into its object domain and must transform *questions of validity* into *questions of behavior*. Thus Luhmann always initiates the reconceptualization of such motions as knowledge and discourse, action and norm, domination and ideological justification, below the threshold of a possible differentiation between the performances of organic systems and of social systems. (In my opinion this is true even of Luhmann's attempt to introduce "sense" and "negation" as differentiating fundamental concepts.) The advantages of a comprehensive conceptual strategy turn into the weaknesses of conceptual imperialism as soon as the steering aspect is rendered independent and the social-scientific object domain is narrowed to potentials for selection.

The conceptual strategy of action theory avoids these weaknesses. However, it produces a dichotomy between normative structures and limiting material conditions.[18] At the analytical level, to be sure, there exists among the subsystems a rank order of socio-cultural, political, and economic systems; but within each of these systems the normative structures must be distinguished from the limiting substratum.

Subsystems	Normative Structures	Substratum Categories
Socio-cultural	status system; subcultural forms of life	distribution of privately available rewards and rights of disposition
Political	political institutions (state)	distribution of legitimate power (and structural force); available organizational rationality
Economic	economic institutions (relations of production)	distribution of economic power (and structural force); available forces of production

This conceptualization requires supplementing the analysis of normative structures with an analysis of limitations and capacities relevant to steering. "Supplementing" is, of course, too weak a requirement for crisis analysis, since what is demanded is a level of analysis at which the *connection* between normative structures and steering problems becomes palpable. I find this level in a historically oriented analysis of social systems, which permits us to ascertain for a given case the range of tolerance within which the goal values of the system might vary without its continued existence being critically endangered. The boundaries of this range of variation are manifested as boundaries of historical continuity.[19] Of course, the flexibility of normative structures—that is, the range of variations that can occur without causing a rupture in tradition—does not depend solely, nor primarily, on consistency requirements of the normative structures themselves. The goal values of social systems are the product, on the one hand, of the cultural values of the constitutive tradition and, on the other, of the non-normative requirements of system integration. In the goal values, the cultural definitions of social life and the survival imperatives that can be reconstructed in systems theory, are connected. Adequate conceptual tools and methods have hitherto been lacking for an analysis of this connection.

Ranges of variation for structural changes obviously can be introduced only within the framework of a theory of social evolution.[20] To do this, the Marxian concept of social formation [*Gesellschaftsformation*] is helpful. The formation of a society is, at any given time, determined by a fundamental principle of organization [*Organizationsprinzip*], which delimits in the abstract the possibilities for alterations of social states. By "principles of organization" I understand highly abstract regulations arising as emergent properties in improbable evolutionary steps and characterizing, at each stage, a new level of development. Organizational principles limit the capacity of a society to learn without losing its identity. According to this definition, steering problems can have crisis effects if (and only if) they cannot be resolved within the range of possibility that is circumscribed by the organizational principle of the society. Principles of organization of this type determine, firstly, the learning mechanism on which the development of productive forces depends; they determine, secondly, the range of variation for the interpretive systems that secure identity; and finally, they fix the institutional boundaries for the possible expansion of steering capacity. Before I illustrate this concept of an organizational principle with a few examples, I would like to justify the choice of the concept with reference to the constituents of social systems.

Chapter 2. *Some Constituents of Social Systems*

To begin with, I shall describe three universal properties of social systems:

a) The exchange between social systems and their environments takes place in production (appropriation of outer nature) and socialization (appropriation of inner nature) through the medium of utterances that admit of truth [*wahrheitsfähiger Äusserungen*] and norms that have need of justification [*rechtfertigungsbedürftiger Normen*]—that is, through discursive validity claims [*Geltungsansprüche*]. In both dimensions, development follows rationally reconstructible patterns.

b) Change in the goal values of social systems is a function of the state of the forces of production and of the degree of system autonomy; but the variation of goal values is limited by a logic of development of world-views [*Weltbilder*] on which the imperatives of system integration have no influence. The socially related [*vergesellschafteten*] individuals form an inner environment that is paradoxical from the point of view of steering.

c) The level of development of a society is determined by the institutionally permitted learning capacity, in particular by whether theoretical-technical and practical questions are differentiated, and whether discursive learning processes can take place.

Re: *a*) The environment of social systems can be divided into three segments: outer nature, or the resources of the non-human environment; the other social systems with which the society is in contact; and inner nature, or the organic substratum of the members of society. Social systems set themselves off symbolically from their social environment. Unless universalistic morals are developed, this can take place in terms of the differentiation between in-group and out-group morality. This problem will not be taken up here. It is the processes with outer and inner nature that are decisive for the specific form in which socio-cultural life reproduces itself. These are processes of adapting to society [Vergesellschaftung] in which the social system "incorporates" nature. Outer nature is appropriated in production processes, inner nature in socialization processes. With developing steering capacity a social system extends its boundaries into nature both without and within. Control over outer nature and integration of inner nature increase with the "power" of the system. Production processes extract natural resources and transform the energies set free into use values. Socialization processes shape the members of the system into subjects capable of speaking and acting. The embryo enters this formative process, and the individual is not released from it until his death (if we disregard pathological cases of desocialization).

Social systems adapt outer nature to society with the help of the forces of production: they organize and train labor power; and develop technologies and strategies. In order to do this they require technically utilizable knowledge. The concepts of cognitive performance and of information that are normally employed in this context suggest too hastily a continuity with the intelligent performances of animals. I see as one of the specific performances of social systems their expansion of control over outer nature through the medium of *utterances that admit of truth*. Work, or instrumental action, is governed by technical rules. The latter incorporate empirical assumptions that imply truth claims, that is, discursively redeemable and fundamentally criticizable claims.

Social systems adapt inner nature to society with the help of normative structures in which needs are interpreted and actions licensed or made obligatory. The concept of motivation that appears here should not conceal the specific fact that social systems accomplish the integration of inner nature through the medium of *norms that have need of justification*. These imply, again, a validity claim that can only be redeemed discursively. To the truth claims that we raise in empirical statements there correspond claims of correctness or appropriateness that we advance with norms of action or of evaluation.

Social systems can maintain themselves *vis-à-vis* outer nature through instrumental actions (according to technical rules), and *vis-à-vis* inner nature through communicative actions (according to valid norms), because at the socio-cultural stage of development animal behavior is reorganized under imperatives of validity claims.[1] This reorganization is effected in structures of linguistically produced intersubjectivity. Linguistic communication has a double structure, for communication about propositional content may take place only with simultaneous metacommunication about interpersonal relations.[2] This is an expression of the specifically human interlacing of cognitive performances and motives for action with linguistic intersubjectivity. Language functions as a kind of transformer; because psychic processes such as sensations, needs and feelings are fitted into structures of linguistic intersubjectivity, inner episodes or experiences are transformed into intentional contents—that is, cognitions into statements, needs and feelings into normative expectations (precepts and values). This transformation produces the distinction, rich in consequences, between the subjectivity of opinion, wanting, pleasure and pain, on the one hand, and the utterances and norms that appear with a *claim to generality* [*Allgemeinheitsanspruch*] on the other. Generality means objectivity of knowledge and legitimacy of valid norms. Both insure the *community or shared meaning* [*Gemeinsamkeit*] that is constitutive for the socio-cultural life-world. The structures of intersubjectivity are just as constitutive for experiences and instrumental action as they are for attitudes and communicative action. These same structures regulate, at the systems level, the control of outer and the integration of inner nature—that is, the processes of adapting to society that, by virtue of the competencies of socially related individuals, operate through the peculiar media of utterances that admit of truth and norms that require justification.

The extension of system autonomy is dependent on developments in the other two dimensions—the development of productive forces (truth) and the alteration of normative structures (correctness/appropriateness). These developments follow rationally reconstructible patterns that are logically independent of one another. The history of secular knowledge and technology is a history of truth-monitored successes in coming to terms with outer nature. It consists of discontinuous but, in the long run, cumulative processes. To explain the world-historically cumulative character of scientific and technical progress, knowledge of empirical mechanisms is necessary but not sufficient. To understand the development of science and technology, we must also conjecture an inner logic through which a hierarchy of non-reversible sequences is fixed from the outset.[3] Limits of a rationally reconstructible pattern of development are reflected in the trivial experience that cognitive advances cannot be simply forgotten as long as the continuity of tradition is unbroken, and that every deviation from the irreversible developmental path is experienced as a regression that exacts its price.

Less trivial is the fact that cultural life is just as little subject to arbitrary definitions. Because the adaptation of inner nature to society also operates through discursive validity claims, alteration of normative structures, as well as the history of science and technology, is a directional process. The integration of inner nature has a cognitive component. In the development from myth, through religion, to philosophy and ideology, the demand for discursive redemption of normative-validity claims increasingly prevails. Like knowledge of nature and technologies, so also world-views follow in their development a pattern that makes it possible to reconstruct rationally the following descriptively enumerated regularities:

—expansion of the secular domain *vis-à-vis* the sphere of the sacred;
—a tendency to develop from far-reaching heteronomy to increasing autonomy;

—the draining of cognitive contents from world-views (from cosmology to the pure system of morals);

—from tribal particularism to universalistic and at the same time individualistic orientations;

—increasing reflexivity of the mode of belief, which can be seen in the sequence: myth as immediately lived system of orientation; teachings; revealed religion; rational religion; ideology.[4]

The components of world-views that secure identity and are efficacious for social integration—that is, moral systems and their accompanying interpretations—follow with increasing complexity a pattern that has a parallel at the ontogenetic level in the logic of the development of moral consciousness. A collectively attained stage of moral consciousness can, as long as the continuity of the tradition endures, just as little be forgotten as can collectively gained knowledge (which does not exclude regression).[5]

Re: *b*) I cannot pursue here the involved interdependencies among possible developments in the spheres of productive forces, steering capacity, and world-views (or moral systems). However, there seems to me to be a conspicuous asymmetry in the form of reproduction of socio-cultural life. While the development of productive forces always extends the scope of contingency of the social system, evolutionary advances in the structures of interpretive systems by no means always offer advantages of selection. Naturally, a growing system autonomy and a corresponding increase in the complexity of the forms of organization of a society can burst normative structures which have become confining and destroy barriers to participation that have become dysfunctional from the point of view of control. This process can be observed today, for example, in the modernization of developing nations. But more problematic cases are also conceivable and require verification. Normative structures can be overturned directly through cognitive dissonances between secular knowledge—expanded with the development of the forces of production—and the dogmatics of traditional world-views. Because the mechanisms which cause developmental advances in the normative structures are independent of the *logic* of their development, there exists *a fortiori* no guarantee that a development of the forces of production and an increase in steering capacity will release exactly those normative alterations that correspond to the steering imperatives of the social system. It is rather an empirical question, whether and to what extent the selection advantage, which a control of outer nature operating through truth claims yields by way of expanded selection potential, will be lost again—in the form of self-produced complexity—through the integration of inner nature operating through claims of correctness and appropriateness. We cannot exclude the possibility that a strengthening of productive forces, which heightens the power of the system, can lead to changes in normative structures that simultaneously restrict the autonomy of the system because they bring forth new legitimacy claims and thereby constrict the range of variation of the goal values. (I will later consider the thesis that precisely this has happened in advanced capitalism because the goal values permitted in the domain of legitimation of a communicative ethic are irreconcilable with an exponential growth of system complexity and, for reasons pertaining to the logic of development, other legitimations cannot be produced.) To the proposition that goal values of social systems vary historically must be added the proposition that *variation* in goal values is limited by a developmental logic of structures of world-views, a logic that *is not at the disposition* of the imperatives of power augmentation.[6]

With this situation is associated a further peculiarity of societies: inner nature does not belong to the system environment in the same way as outer nature. On the one hand, as we can study in the psychosomatics of disturbed organic processes,[7] organic substrata of socially related individuals are not simply external to the social system; on the other hand, inner nature remains, *after* its integration into the social system, something like an inner environment, since socially related individuals resist, to the extent of their individuation, being absorbed without remainder into society. Socialization, the adapting of inner nature to society, unlike production, the adapting of outer nature to society, cannot be satisfactorily conceived of as a reduction of environmental complexity. While the freedom of movement of the system normally expands with the reduction of environmental complexity, a progressive adaptation of inner nature to society rather narrows the scope of contingency of the system. With growing individuation, the immunization of socialized individuals against decisions of the differentiated control center seems to gain in strength. The normative structures become effective as a kind of self-inhibiting mechanism *vis-à-vis* imperatives of power expansion. In the framework of the logic of self-regulating systems, this can only be expressed as follows: inner nature is at once a system environment and a system element. His own nature is given to the subject capable of speaking and acting in the same paradoxical way—as body and as material substance.[8] It is, of course, my opinion that these paradoxes indicate only the blurring of an overextended systems theory. They disappear when one chooses, not system and self-steering, but life-world and intersubjectivity as the superordinate point of view, and therefore conceives socialization *from the outset* as individuation. This connection can be conceived of in the theory of language, while it leads only to absurdities if one sticks obstinately to systems theory.[9] Societies are *also* systems, but their mode of development does not follow solely the logic of the expansion of system autonomy (power); social evolution transpires rather within the bounds of a logic of the life-world, the structures of which are determined by linguistically produced intersubjectivity and are based on criticizable validity claims.

Re: *c*) If I have correctly described the constituents of social systems, steering capacity changes as a function of growing control over outer nature and of increasing integration of inner nature. Evolution in both dimensions takes place in the form of directional learning processes that work through discursively redeemable validity claims. The development of productive forces and the alteration of normative structures follow, respectively, logics of growing theoretical and practical insight.[10] Of course, the rationally reconstructible patterns that collective learning processes follow— that is, the history of secular knowledge and technology on the one hand and of the structural alteration of identity-securing interpretive systems on the other—explain only the logically necessary sequence of *possible* developments. The *actual* developments, innovations and stagnations, occurrence of crises, productive or unproductive working out of crises, and so on can be explained only with the aid of empirical mechanisms. It is my conjecture that the fundamental mechanism for social evolution in general is to be found in an automatic inability not to learn. Not *learning*, but *not-learning* is the phenomenon that calls for explanation at the socio-cultural stage of development. Therein lies, if you will, the rationality of man. Only against this background does the overpowering irrationality of the history of the species become visible.

Formal viewpoints for demarcating different levels of learning follow from the fact that we learn in two dimensions (theoretical and practical) and that these learning processes are connected with validity claims that can be discursively redeemed. *Non-reflexive learning* takes place in action contexts in which implicitly raised theoretical and practical validity claims are naively taken for granted and accepted or rejected without discursive consideration. *Reflexive learning* takes place through discourses in which we thematize practical validity claims that have become problematic or have been rendered problematic through institutionalized doubt, and redeem or dismiss them on the basis of arguments. The level of learning which a social formation makes possible could depend upon whether the organizational principle of the society permits (*a*) differentiation between theoretical and practical questions and (*b*) transition from non-reflexive (prescientific) to reflexive learning. From these alternatives there follow four possible combinations, of which, if I am correct, three have been historically realized.

| | Theoretical and Practical Questions Are | |
Learning	*Not Differentiated*	*Differentiated*
Non-reflexive	X	——
Reflexive	X	X

This schema is, of course, inadequate, even for purposes of a rough approximation, because it carries over concepts developed in a logic of discourse (theoretical/practical)[11] into heterogeneous interpretive systems; in addition, it does not specify whether theoretical and practical questions remain unseparated only within the ruling interpretive framework or also in life-practice. From magical and animistic world-views, we can infer a life-practice that ignores this difference, while mythical world-views co-exist with secular knowledge that is assimilated and extended into spheres of social labor. Thus, in the latter case, the distinction between technically utilizable knowledge (admitting of theory) and the practically relevant interpretation of the natural and social life-world has actually already taken place. Furthermore, the schema does not delineate areas that are rendered accessible to institutionalized partial discourse. With the rise of philosophy, the elements of mythical traditions were for the first time freed for discursive consideration; but classical philosophy conceived and treated practically relevant interpretations as theoretical questions, while it devalued, as inaccessible to theory, technically utilizable knowledge. With the rise of modern science, on the other hand, precisely this sphere of empirical knowledge was drawn into reflexive learning processes. At the same time, in philosophy there prevailed a tendency, leading to positivism, to differentiate theoretical and practical questions according to their logical form; however, the aim was to exclude practical questions from discourse. They are no longer thought to be "susceptible of truth." [12] In contrast, the institutionalization of general practical discourse would introduce a new stage of learning for society.

If the determinations provisionally introduced in *a)* through *c)* define the constituents of social systems, then it seems sensible to look for organizational principles that determine the learning capacity, and thus the level of development, of a society—above all in regard to its forces of production and its identity-securing interpretive systems—and which thereby limit the possible growth in steering capabilities as well. Marx determined different social formations in terms of the command of the means of production, that is, as *relations of production.* He placed the nucleus that organizes the whole at a level at which normative structures are interlaced with the material substratum. If the relations of production are to represent the organizing principles of society, they may not, of course, be equated with the determinate forms of ownership at any given time. Organizational principles are highly abstract regulations that define ranges of possibility. Moreover, to speak of the relations of production misleadingly suggests a narrow economistic interpretation. Which subsystem can assume functional primacy in a society[13]—and thus the guidance of social evolution—is, however, first established by its principle of organization.

Chapter 3. Illustration of Social Principles of Organization

I think it meaningful to distinguish four social formations: primitive [vorhochkulterelle], traditional, capitalist, post-capitalist.[1] Except for primitive societies, we are dealing with class societies. (I designate state-socialist societies—in view of their political-elitist disposition of the means of production—as "post-capitalist class societies.")

Social Formations

	Primitive
	Civilizations
	Traditional
	Modern
Class Societies	Capitalist
	liberal capitalist
	organized or advanced capitalist
	Post-capitalist
	Post-modern

(handwritten marginalia: "why does he exclude post-capitalist "formation"? cultures?"; "Post-capitalist — State-Socialism?"; "Post-modern — not a class society.")

The interest behind the examination of crisis tendencies in late- and post-capitalist class societies is in exploring the possibilities of a "post-modern" society—that is, a historically new principle of organization and not a different name for the surprising vigor of an aged capitalism.[2] I would like to illustrate what is meant by social principles of organization and how definite types of crisis can be derived from them in terms of three social formations. These loose remarks are intended neither to simulate nor to substitute for a theory of social evolution. They serve solely to introduce a concept by way of examples. For each of the three social formations I shall sketch the determining principle of organization, indicate the possibilities it opens to social evolution, and infer the type of crisis it allows. Without a theory of social evolution to rely on, principles of organization cannot be grasped abstractly, but only picked out inductively and elaborated with reference to the institutional sphere (kinship system, political system, economic system) that possesses functional primacy for a given stage of development.

Primitive Social Formation. The primary roles of age and sex form *the organizational principle* of primitive societies.[3] The institutional core is the *kinship system*, which at this stage of development represents a total institution; family structures determine the totality of social intercourse. They simultaneously secure social and system integration. World-views and norms are scarcely differentiated from one another; both are built around rituals and taboos that require no independent sanctions. This principle of organization is compatible only with familial and tribal morals. Vertical or horizontal social relations that overstep the bounds of the kinship system are not possible. In societies organized along kinship lines, the forces of production cannot be augmented through exploitation of labor power (raising the rate of exploitation through physical force). The learning mechanism, which is built into the behavioral system of instrumental action [*Funktionskreis instrumentalen Handelns*],[4] leads, over long periods, to a seemingly ordered sequence of less fundamental innovations.[5] At the stage of development of primitive society, there seems to be no systematic motive for producing more goods than are necessary to satisfy basic needs, even though the state of the productive forces may permit a surplus.[6] Since no contradictory imperatives follow from this principle of organization, it is external change that overloads the narrowly limited steering capacity of societies organized along kinship lines and undermines the familial and tribal identities. The usual source of change is demographic growth in connection with ecological factors—above all, interethnic dependency as a result of economic exchange, war, and conquest.[7]

Traditional Social Formation. The *principle of organization* is *class domination* [*Klassenherrschaft*] in political form.[8] With the rise of a bureaucratic apparatus of authority, a control center is differentiated out of the kinship system. This allows the transference of the production and distribution of social wealth from familial forms of organization to ownership of the means of production. The kinship system is no longer the institutional nucleus of the whole system; it surrenders the central functions of power and control to the state. This is the beginning of a functional specification and autonomization, in the course of which the family loses all of its economic functions and some of its socializing functions. At this stage of development, subsystems arise that serve predominantly either system or social integration. At their point of intersection lies the legal order that regulates the privilege of disposition of the means of production and the strategic exercise of power, which, in turn, requires legitimation. To the differentiation between the authority apparatus and the legal order on the one side, and the counterfactual justifications and moral systems on the other, there corresponds the institutional separation of secular and sacred powers.

The new organizational principle permits a significant strengthening of system autonomy. It presupposes functional differentiation and makes possible the formation of generalized media (power and money) as well as reflexive mechanisms (positive law). But this latitude for growth in steering capacity is developed at the cost of a fundamentally unstable class structure. With private ownership of the means of production, a power relationship is institutionalized in class societies, which in the long run threatens social integration;[9] for the opposition of interests established in the class relationship represents a conflict potential. Of course, within the framework of a legitimate order of authority, the opposition of interests can be kept latent and integrated for a certain time. This is the achievement of legitimating world-views or ideologies. They remove the counterfactual validity claims of normative structures from the sphere of public thematization and testing. The order of authority is justified by falling back on traditional world-views and a conventional civic ethic.

In spite of considerable vertical differentiation, the new organizational principle holds horizontal social relations through unpolitical exchange relations (local markets, city-country) within narrow limits. The political class rule requires a mediation of tribal morals through civic ethics that remain dependent on tradition—that is, particularistic. It is incompatible with universalistic forms of intercourse. In a class system of social labor, the forces of production can be augmented through raising the rate of exploitation, that is, through organized forced labor. Thus a socially produced surplus product arises that is appropriated according to privilege. The enhancing of the productive force has its limits, to be sure, in the persistence of unplanned, nature-like development [*Naturwüchsigkeit*] of technical innovations. (Technically utilizable knowledge is not extended through reflexive learning.)[10]

In traditional societies the type of crisis that arises proceeds from internal contradictions. The contradiction exists between validity claims of systems of norms and justifications that cannot explicitly permit exploitation, and a class structure in which privileged appropriation of socially produced wealth is the rule. The problem of how socially produced wealth may be inequitably, and yet legitimately, distributed is temporarily solved through the ideological protection of counterfactual validity claims. In critical situations, traditional societies extend the scope of their control through heightened exploitation of labor power; that is, they augment power either directly through heightened physical force (of which the history of penal law gives good indicators), or indirectly through generalization of forced payments (in the sequence of work-, product-, and money-rents). Consequently, crises as a rule issue from steering problems that necessitate a strengthening of system autonomy through heightened repression. The latter leads in turn to legitimation losses, which for their part result in class struggles (often in connection with foreign conflicts). Class struggles finally threaten social integration and can lead to an overthrow of the political system and to new foundations of legitimation—that is, to a new group identity.

Liberal-Capitalist Social Formation. The *principle of organization* is the *relationship of wage labor and capital,* which is anchored in the system of bourgeois civil law. With the rise of a sphere, free of the state, of commerce between private autonomous owners of commodities—that is, with the institutionalization in independent states of goods-, capital-, and labor-markets and the establishment of world trade—"civil society" [*bürgerliche Gesellschaft*] [11] is differentiated out of the political-economic system. This signifies a depoliticization of the class relationship and an anonymization of class domination. The state and the politically constituted system of social labor are no longer the institutional nucleus of the system as a whole. Instead, the modern rational state—whose prototype Max Weber analyzed [12]—becomes the complementary arrangement to self-regulative market commerce.[13] Externally, the state still insures by political means the territorial integrity and the competitiveness of the domestic economy. Internally, the previously dominant medium of control, legitimate power, serves above all to maintain the general conditions of production, which make possible the market-regulated process of capital realization. Economic exchange becomes the dominant steering medium. After the capitalist mode of production has been established, the exercise of the state's power within the social system can be limited: (a) to the protection of bourgeois commerce in accord with civil law (police and administration of justice); (b) to the shielding of the market mechanism from self-destructive side effects (for example, legislation for the protection of labor); (c) to the satisfaction of the prerequisites of production in the economy as a whole (public school education, transportation, and communication); and (d) to the adaptation of the system of civil law to needs that arise from the process of accumulation (tax, banking, and business law).[14] By fulfilling these four classes of tasks, the state secures the structural prerequisites of the reproduction process as capitalistic.

Although in traditional societies an institutional differentiation between spheres of system integration and social integration had already set in, the economic system remained dependent on the supply of legitimation from the socio-cultural system. Only the relative uncoupling of the economic system from the political permits a sphere to arise in bourgeois society that is free from the traditional ties and given over to the strategic-utilitarian action orientations of market participants. Competing entrepreneurs then make their decisions according to maxims of profit-oriented competition and replace value-oriented with interest-guided action.[15]

The new organizational principle opens a broad scope for the development of productive forces and of normative structures. With the imperatives of the self-realization of capital, the mode of production sets in motion an expanded reproduction that is tied to the mechanism of innovations that enhance labor productivity. As soon as the limits of physical exploitation—that is, of raising the absolute surplus value—are reached, the accumulation of capital necessitates development of technical productive forces and, in this way, coupling of technically utilizable knowledge to reflexive learning processes. On the other hand, the now autonomous economic exchange relieves the political order of the pressures of legitimation. Self-regulative market commerce requires supplementation, not only through rational state administration and abstract law, but through a strategic-utilitarian morality in the sphere of social labor, which in the private domain is equally compatible with a "Protestant" or a "formalistic" ethic. Bourgeois ideologies can assume a universalistic structure and appeal to generalizable interests because the property order has shed its political form and been converted into a relation of production that, it seems, can legitimate itself. The institution of the market can be founded on the justice inherent in the exchange of equivalents; and, for this reason, the bourgeois constitutional state finds its justification in the legitimate relations of production. This is the message of rational natural law since Locke. The relations of production can do without a traditional authority legitimated from above.

Of course, the socially integrative effect of the value form may be restricted, by and large, to the bourgeois class. The loyalty and subordination of members of the new urban proletariat, recruited mainly from the ranks of the peasants, are certainly maintained more through a mixture of traditionalistic ties, fatalistic willingness to follow, lack of perspective, and naked repression than through the convincing force of bourgeois ideologies. This does not diminish the socially integrative significance of this new type of ideology in a society that no longer recognizes political domination in personal form.[16]

With the political anonymization of class rule, the socially dominant class must convince itself that it no longer rules. Universalistic bourgeois ideologies can fulfill this task insofar as they (*a*) are founded "scientifically" on the critique of tradition and (*b*) possess the character of a model, that is, anticipate a state of society whose possibility need not from the start be denied by a dynamically growing economic society. All the more sensitively, however, must bourgeois society react to the evident contradiction between idea and reality. For this reason the critique of bourgeois society could take the form of an unmasking of bourgeois ideologies themselves by confronting idea and reality. The achievement of the capitalist principle of organization is nevertheless extraordinary. It not only frees the economic system, uncoupled from the political system, from the legitimations of the socially integrative subsystems, but enables it, along with its system integrative tasks, to make a contribution to social integration. With these achievements, the susceptibility of the social system to crisis certainly grows, as steering problems can now become *directly* threatening to identity. In this sense I would like to speak of *system crises*.

In an unplanned, nature-like [*naturwüchsig*] movement of economic development, the organizational principle sets no limits to the development of productive forces. The normative structures also obtain a broad scope for development, for the new principle of organization permits (for the first time) universalistic value systems. It is, of course, incompatible with a communicative ethic, which requires not only generality of norms but a discursively attained consensus about the *generalizability* of the normatively prescribed interests. The principle of organization transposes the conflict potential of class opposition into the steering dimension, where it expresses itself in the form of economic crises. For liberal capitalism, the fluctuation of prosperity, crisis, and depression is typical. The opposition of interests, which is grounded in the relation of wage labor and capital, comes to light, not directly in class conflicts, but in the interruption of the process of accumulation, that is, in the form of steering problems. A general concept of system crisis can be gained from the logic of this economic crisis.

The following schema sums up the connections between the organizational principles introduced as examples and the corresponding types of crisis.

In determining the possibilities for evolution in each of the three developmental dimensions (production, steering, and socialization), the principle of organization determines whether, and if so, (*a*) how system and social integration can be functionally differentiated; (*b*) when dangers to system integration must result in dangers to social

Social Formations	Principle of Organization	Social and System Integration	Type of Crisis
Primitive	kinship relations: primary roles (age, sex)	no differentiation between social and system integration	externally induced identity crisis
Traditional	political class rule: state power and socio-economic classes	functional differentiation between social and system integration	internally determined identity crisis
Liberal-capitalist	unpolitical class rule: wage labor and capital	system integrative economic system also takes over socially integrative tasks	system crisis

handwritten margin notes: (Authority) opposition of interests introduced

integration, that is crises; and (*c*) in what way steering problems are transformed into dangers to identity, that is, what type of crisis predominates.

Chapter 4.   System Crisis Elucidated Through the Example of the Liberal-Capitalist Crisis Cycle

In liberal capitalism, crises appear *in the form* of unresolved economic steering problems. Dangers to system integration *are* direct threats to social integration, so that we are justified in speaking of economic crisis. In primitive social formations, a similarly close association exists, for the familial principle of organization does not permit separation of system and social integration. Functional differentiation, which developed in traditional societies, is not revoked in the transition to the modern. But in liberal capitalism, there occurs a peculiar transfer of socially integrative tasks to the separate, unpolitical steering system of the market in such a way that the elements of tradition that are effective (at first for the middle class) for legitimation (rational-natural law, utilitarianism) become dependent on an ideology that is itself built into the economic basis—namely, the exchange of equivalents. In traditional societies, crises appear when, and only when, steering problems cannot be resolved within the possibility space circumscribed by the principle of organization and therefore produce dangers to system integration that threaten the identity of the society. In liberal-capitalist societies, on the other hand, crises become endemic because temporarily unresolved steering problems, which the process of economic growth produces at more or less regular intervals, *as such* endanger social integration. With the persistent instability of accelerated social change, periodically recurring, socially disintegrating steering problems produce the objective foundation for a crisis consciousness in the bourgeois class and for revolutionary hopes among wage laborers. No previous social formation lived so much in fear and expectation of a sudden system change, even though the idea of a temporally condensed transformation—that is, of a revolutionary leap—is oddly in contrast to the form of motion of system crisis as a permanent crisis [*Dauerkrise*].

The transfer of socially integrative functions to a subsystem that primarily fulfills system integrative functions is possible only because in liberal capitalism the class relationship is institutionalized through the labor market and is thereby depoliticized. Since the source of social wealth—that is, the labor power of the worker—becomes a commodity, and social capital is reproduced under conditions of wage labor, labor and exchange processes take on the double character analyzed by Marx: in producing use values, labor processes serve to produce exchange values. By regulating the allocation of labor power and of goods through the money mechanism, exchange processes serve the formation and self-realization of capital. The market thereby assumes a double function: on the one hand, it functions as a steering mechanism in the system of social labor, which is controlled through the medium of money; on the other, it institutionalizes a power relation between owners of the means of production and wage laborers. Because the *social power* of the capitalist is institutionalized as an exchange relation in the form of the private labor contract and the siphoning off of privately available surplus value has replaced *political dependency*, the market assumes, together with its cybernetic function, an ideological function. The class relationship can assume the anonymous, unpolitical form of wage dependency. In Marx, therefore, theoretical analysis of the value form has the double task of uncovering both the steering principle of commerce in a market economy and the basic ideology of bourgeois class society. The theory of value serves, at the same time, the functional analysis of the economic system and the critique of ideology of a class domination that can be unmasked, even for the bourgeois consciousness, through the proof that in the labor market equivalents are not exchanged. The market secures for the owners of the means of production the power, sanctioned in civil law, to appropriate surplus value and to use it privately and autonomously. Naturally, in its crisis-ridden course, the process of accumulation surrenders the secret of the "contradiction" embedded in this mode of production. Economic growth takes place through periodically recurring crises because the class structure, transplanted into the economic steering system, has transformed *the contradiction of class interests into a contradiction of system imperatives*. In choosing this formulation we employ the concept of contradiction in two different theoretical frameworks. In order to prevent misunderstandings, I would like to insert a conceptual clarification.

The concept of contradiction has undergone such attrition that it is often used synonymously with "antagonism," "opposition," or "conflict." According to Hegel and Marx, however, "conflicts" are only the form of appearance, the empirical side of a fundamentally logical contradiction. Conflicts can be comprehended only with reference to the operatively effective rules according to which incompatible claims or intentions are produced within an action system. But "contradictions" cannot exist between claims or intentions in the same sense as they can between statements; the system of rules according to which utterances [*Äusserungen*]—that is, opinions and actions in which intentions are incorporated—are produced is obviously different in kind from the system of rules according to which we form statements and transform them without affecting their truth value. In other words, the deep structures of a society are not logical structures in a narrow sense. Propositional contents, on the other hand, are always used in utterances. The logic that could justify speaking of "social contradictions" would therefore have to be a logic of the employment of propositional contents in speech and in action. It would have to extend to communicative relations between subjects capable of speaking and acting; it would have to be universal pragmatics rather than logic.[1]

We can speak of the "fundamental contradiction" of a social formation when, and only when, its organizational principle necessitates that individuals and groups repeatedly confront one another with claims and intentions that are, in the long run, incompatible. In class societies this is the case. As long as the incompatibility of claims and intentions is not recognized by the participants, the conflict remains latent. Such forcefully integrated action systems are, of course, in need of an ideological justification to conceal the asymmetrical distribution of chances for the legitimate satisfaction of needs (that is, repression of needs). Communication between participants is then systematically distorted or blocked. Under conditions of forceful integration, the contradiction cannot be *identified* as a contradiction between the *declared* intentions of hostile parties and be settled in strategic action. Instead, it assumes the ideological form of a contradiction between the intentions that subjects believe themselves to be carrying out and their, as we say, unconscious motives or fundamental interests. As soon as incompatibility becomes conscious, conflict becomes manifest, and irreconcilable interests are recognized as antagonistic interests.[2]

Systems theory, too, is concerned with the logic of a system of rules according to which incompatibilities can be produced. When more problems are posed in a given environment than the system's steering capacity can solve, logically derivable contradictions appear that require, on pain of ruin, an alteration of system structures—alteration or surrender of elements that up to that point belonged to its "structural continuity" [*Bestand*]. These "contradictions" are introduced with reference to problems of system maintenance [*Bestandserhaltungsprobleme*]. They are not, therefore, as are dialectical contradictions, related from the start to communicative relations between subjects or groups of subjects capable of speaking and acting. Within the framework of systems theory, conflicts can be seen as the expression of unresolved systemic problems. But the continued employment of the term "contradiction" should not obscure the differences between the logic of self-regulated systems and the logic of ordinary language communication.

Conflicts that are described independently of communications theory or systems theory are empirical phenomena without relation to truth. Only when we conceive of such oppositions within communications theory or systems theory do they take on an immanent relation to logical categories. Problems of system integration admit of truth insofar as they are defined by a finite number of specifiable (and functionally equivalent) solutions. Naturally the truth relation of steering problems exists primarily for the observer (or systems theorist) and not necessarily for the participants of the action system in question. Problems of social integration (as whose expression conflicts can be conceived) likewise admit of truth; for competing claims can be understood as recommendations of (and warnings against) commonly binding norms of action on whose competing validity claims judgment could be passed in practical discourse. But the truth relation of systematically produced conflicts of interest exists, in this case, not for the sociologist, but for the members of the action system under analysis. In contrast to systems analysis, then, critique is related to the consciousness of addressees susceptible of enlightenment.[3]

The class structure determines which contradictions follow from the privileged appropriation of socially produced wealth. In traditional societies, such contradictions are manifested directly at the level of opposition of the interests of acting parties. In liberal capitalism, the class antagonism is reflected at the level of steering problems. The dynamic aspect thereby comes to the fore. Since, in the capitalist mode of production, the society acquires the capability to develop the forces of production relatively constantly, economic crisis designates the pattern of *a crisis-ridden course of economic growth.*

The accumulation of capital is, if we follow Marx's analysis, tied to the appropriation of surplus value. This means that economic growth is regulated through a mechanism that establishes and at the same time partially conceals a relation of social power. Because the production of value is controlled through the private appropriation of surplus value, a spiral of contradictions results that can be reconstructed within systems theory. The accumulation of total capital involves periodic devaluations of elements of capital. This form of development is the crisis cycle. *Under the aspect of the accumulation of capital,* the self-negating pattern of development is represented in such a way that, on the one hand, the mass of exchange and use values (that is capital and social wealth) accumulates by raising the relative surplus value, that is, by way of technical progress that is capital intensive and that, at the same time, cuts down expenses. But, on the other hand, at each new stage of accumulation, the composition of capital alters to the detriment of variable capital, which is alone productive of surplus value. From this analysis Marx derives the tendency to a falling rate of profit and the weakening impulse to continuation of the process of accumulation.

Under the aspect of the realization of capital, the same contradiction is represented in such a way that at each new stage of accumulation potential social wealth grows along with the increase in surplus value. On the other hand, however, the power of consumption of the masses, and therefore the chance to realize capital, can be strengthened to the same extent only if the owners of capital relinquish corresponding portions of their own surplus value. Hence, the process of accumulation must come to a standstill because of lack of *possibilities* of realization or because of lack of incentives to invest.

The interruption of the process of accumulation assumes the form of capital destruction. This is the economic form of appearance of the real social process that expropriates individual capitalists (competition) and deprives the laboring masses of their means of subsistence (unemployment). Economic crisis is immediately transformed into social crisis; for, in unmasking the opposition of social classes, it provides a practical critique of ideology of the market's pretension to be free of power. The economic crisis results from contradictory system imperatives and threatens social integration. It is, *at the same time,* a social crisis in which the interests of acting groups collide and place in question the social integration of the society.

The economic crisis is the first (and perhaps only) example in world history of a system crisis characterized in the following way: namely, that the dialectical contradiction between members of an interaction context comes to pass *in terms of* structurally insoluble system contradictions or steering problems. Through this displacement of conflicts of interest to the level of system steering, systems crises gain an objectivity rich in contrast. They have the appearance of natural catastrophes that break forth from the center of a system of purposive rational action. While in traditional societies antagonisms between social classes were mediated through ideological forms of consciousness and thus had *the fateful objectivity of a context of delusion* [*schicksalhafte Objektivität eines Verblendungszusammenhang*], in liberal capitalism, class antagonism is shifted from the intersubjectivity of the life-world into the substratum of this world. Commodity fetishism is both a secularized residual ideology and the actually functioning steering principle of the economic system. Economic crises thus lose the character of a fate accessible to self-reflection and acquire *the objectivity of inexplicable, contingent, natural events.* The ideological core has thus shifted to ground level. Before it can be destroyed by reflection, these events are in need of an objective examination of system processes. This need is reflected in the Marxian critique of political economy.[4]

Although the theory of value is also intended to fulfill the task of a critique of commodity fetishism—and of the derivative cultural phenomena of bourgeois society[5]—it is directly a systems analysis of the economic process of reproduction. The fundamental categories of the theory of value are thereby set up in such a way that propositions that follow from a theory of contradictory capital accumulation can be transformed into action-theoretic assumptions of the theory of classes. Marx holds open for himself the possibility of retranslating the economic processes of capital utilization, which take place within the bounds of class structure, into social processes between classes—after all, he is the author of the *Eighteenth Brumaire* as well as of *Capital.* It is precisely this sociological retranslation of an economic analysis that proceeds immanently that gives rise to difficulties in the altered conditions of organized capitalism. I would like to take up the not-yet-satisfactorily-answered question Has capitalism changed?[6] in the form: Is the fundamental contradiction of the capitalist social formation effective in the same way under the forms of appearance of organized capitalism, or has the logic of crisis changed? Has capitalism been fully transformed into a post-capitalist social formation that has overcome the crisis-ridden form of economic growth?

thus, w/ liberal-Capitalism, we have the beginnings of system crisis in the form of economic crisis

PART II. Crisis Tendencies in
Advanced Capitalism

I must neglect here the very complex transition from liberal to
organized capitalism,[1] which took place in interesting national
variations, and limit myself to a *model* of the most important
structural features of organized capitalism (Chapter 1) in order to
derive from them the possible classes of crisis tendencies that *can*
arise in this social formation (Chapters 2 and 3). It is not easy to
determine empirically the probability of boundary conditions under
which the *possible* crisis tendencies *actually* set in and prevail. The
empirical indicators we have at our disposal are as yet inadequate. I
will therefore limit myself to a presentation of important arguments
and counterarguments (Chapters 4–7). It goes without saying that
this argumentation sketch cannot replace empirical investigations,
but can at best guide them.

Chapter 1. A Descriptive Model of Advanced Capitalism

The expression "organized or state-regulated capitalism" refers to
two classes of phenomena, both of which can be attributed to the
advanced stage of the accumulation process. It refers, on the one
hand, to the process of economic concentration—the rise of
national and, subsequently, of multinational corporations[2]—and to
the organization of markets for goods, capital, and labor. On the
other hand, it refers to the fact that the state intervenes in the
market as functional gaps develop. The spread of oligopolistic
market structures certainly means the end of *competitive capitalism.* But however much companies broaden their temporal perspectives and expand control over their environments, the steering
mechanism of the market remains in force as long as investment
decisions are made according to criteria of company profits.
Similarly, the supplementation and partial replacement of the
market mechanism by state intervention marks the end of *liberal*

capitalism. Nonetheless, no matter how much the scope of the private autonomous commerce of commodity owners is administratively restricted, political planning of the allocation of scarce resources does not occur as long as the priorities of the society as a whole develop in an unplanned, nature-like manner—that is, as secondary effects of the strategies of private enterprise. In advanced-capitalist societies the economic, the administrative, and the legitimation systems can be characterized, approximately and at a very general level, as follows.

The Economic System. During the sixties, various authors, using the United States as an example, developed a three-sector model based on the distinction between the private and the public sectors.[3] According to the model, private production is market-oriented, one sub-sector still being regulated by competition while the other is determined by the market strategies of oligopolies that tolerate a "competitive fringe." By contrast, in the public sector, especially in the armaments and space-travel industries, huge concerns have arisen whose investment decisions can be made almost without regard for the market. These concerns are either enterprises directly controlled by the state or private firms living on government contracts. In the monopolistic and the public sectors, capital-intensive industries predominate; in the competitive sector, labor-intensive industries predominate. In the monopolistic and public sectors, companies are faced with strong unions. In the competitive sector workers are less well organized, and wage levels are correspondingly different. In the monopolistic sector, we can observe relatively rapid advances in production. In the public sector, companies do not need to be rationalized to the same extent. In the competitive sector, they cannot be.[4]

The Administrative System. The state apparatus carries out numerous imperatives of the economic system. These can be ordered from two perspectives: by means of global planning, it regulates the economic cycle as a whole; and it creates and improves conditions for utilizing excess accumulated capital. Global planning is limited by the private autonomous disposition of the means of production (for the investment freedom of private enterprises cannot be restricted) and positively by the avoidance of instabilities. To this extent, the fiscal and financial regulation of the business cycle, as well as individual measures intended to regulate investment and overall demand—credits, price guarantees, subsidies, loans, secondary redistribution of income, government contracts guided by business-cycle policy, indirect labor-market policy, etc.—have the reactive character of avoidance strategies within the framework of a system of goals. This system is determined by a formulistically [*leerformelhaft*] demanded adjustment between competing imperatives of steady growth, stability of the currency, full employment, and balance of foreign trade.

While global planning manipulates the boundary conditions of decisions made by private enterprise in order to correct the market mechanism with respect to dysfunctional secondary effects the state actually *replaces* the market mechanism whenever it creates and improves conditions for the realization of capital:

—through "strengthening the competitive capability of the nation" by organizing supranational economic blocks, securing international stratification by imperialist means, etc.;

—through unproductive government consumption (for example, armaments and space exploration);

—through guiding, in accord with structural policy, the flow of capital into sectors neglected by an autonomous market;

—through improvement of the material infrastructure (transportation, education, health, recreation, urban and regional planning, housing construction, etc.);

—through improvement of the immaterial infrastructure (general promotion of science, investments in research and development, provision of patents, etc.);

—through heightening the productivity of human labor (general system of education, vocational schools, programs for training and re-education, etc.);

—through relieving the social and material costs resulting from private production (unemployment compensation, welfare, repair of ecological damage).

Improving the nation's position in the international market, government demand for unproductive commodities, and measures for guiding the flow of capital, open up or improve chances for capital investment. With all but the last of the remaining measures this is indeed a concomitant phenomenon; but the goal is to increase the productivity of labor and thereby the "use value" of capital (through provision of collective commodities and through qualification of labor power).

The Legitimation System. With the appearance of functional weaknesses in the market and dysfunctional side effects of the steering mechanism, the basic bourgeois ideology of fair exchange collapses. Re-coupling the economic system to the political—which in a way repoliticizes the relations of production—creates an increased need for legitimation. The state apparatus no longer, as in liberal capitalism, merely secures the general conditions of production (in the sense of the prerequisites for the continued existence of the reproduction process), but is now actively engaged in it. It must, therefore—like the pre-capitalist state—be legitimated, although it can no longer rely on residues of tradition that have been undermined and worn out during the development of capitalism. Moreover, through the universalistic value-systems of bourgeois ideology, civil rights—including the right to participate in political elections—have become established; and legitimation can be disassociated from the mechanism of elections only temporarily and under extraordinary conditions. This problem is resolved through a system of formal democracy. Genuine participation of citizens in the processes of political will-formation [*politischen Willensbildungsprozessen*],[5] that is, substantive democracy, would bring to consciousness the contradiction between administratively socialized production and the continued private appropriation and use of surplus value. In order to keep this contradiction from being thematized, then the administrative system must be sufficiently independent of legitimating will-formation.

The arrangement of formal democratic institutions and procedures permits administrative decisions to be made largely independently of specific motives of the citizens. This takes place through a legitimation process that elicits generalized motives—that is, diffuse mass loyalty—but avoids participation.[6] This structural alteration of the bourgeois public realm [*Öffentlichkeit*] provides for application of institutions and procedures that are democratic in form, while the citizenry, in the midst of an objectively [*an sich*] political society, enjoy the status of passive citizens with only the right to withhold acclamation.[7] Private autonomous investment decisions thus have their necessary complement in the civic privatism of the civil public.

In the structurally depoliticized public realm, the need for legitimation is reduced to two residual requirements: The first, civic privatism—that is, political abstinence combined with an orientation to career, leisure, and consumption (see Part II, Chapter 7)—promotes the expectation of suitable rewards within the system (money, leisure time, and security). This privatism is taken into account by a welfare-state substitute program, which also incorporates elements of an achievement ideology transferred to the educational system.[8] Secondly, the structural depoliticization itself requires justification, which is supplied either by democratic elite theories (which go back to Schumpeter[9] and Max Weber) or by technocratic systems theories (which go back to the institutionalism of the twenties).[10] In the history of bourgeois social science, these theories today have a function similar to that of the classical doctrine of political economy. In earlier phases of capitalist development, the latter doctrine suggested the "naturalness" of the capitalist economic society.

Class Structure. While the political form of the relations of production in traditional societies permitted easy identification of ruling groups, in liberal capitalism manifest domination was replaced by the politically anonymous power of civil subjects. (Of course, during economically induced social crises these anonymous powers again assumed the identifiable form of a political adversary, as can be seen in the fronts of the European labor movement.) But, while in organized capitalism the relations of production are indeed repoliticized to a certain extent, the political form of the class relationship is not thereby restored. Instead, the political anonymity of class domination is superseded by social anonymity. That is, the structures of advanced capitalism can be understood as reaction formations to endemic crisis. To ward off system crisis, advanced-capitalist societies focus all forces of social integration at the point of the structurally most probable conflict—in order all the more effectively to keep it latent.[11] At the same time, in doing so they satisfy the political demands of reformist labor parties.[12]

In this connection, the quasi-political wage structure, which depends on negotiations between companies and unions, plays a historically epochmaking role. "Price setting" [*Machtpreisbildung*, W. Hofmann], which replaces price competition in the oligopolistic markets, has its counterpart in the labor market. Just as the great concerns quasi-administratively control price movements in their markets, so too, on the other side, they obtain quasi-political compromises with union adversaries on wage movements. In those branches of industry belonging to the monopolistic and the public sectors, which are central to economic development, the commodity called labor power receives a "political price." The "wage-scale partners" [*Tarifpartner*] find a broad zone of compromise, since increased labor costs can be passed on through prices and since there is a convergence of the middle-range demands of both sides on the state—demands that aim at increasing productivity, qualifying labor power, and improving the social situation of the workers.[13] The monopolistic sector can, as it were, externalize class conflict.

The consequences of this immunization of the original conflict zone are: (*a*) disparate wage developments and/or a sharpening of wage disputes in the public service sector;[14] (*b*) permanent inflation, with corresponding temporary redistribution of income to the disadvantage of unorganized workers and other marginal groups; (*c*) permanent crisis in government finances, together with public poverty (that is, impoverishment of public transportation, education, housing and health care); and (*d*) an inadequate adjustment of disproportional economic developments, sectoral (agriculture) as well as regional (marginal areas).[15]

In the decades since World War II the most advanced capitalist countries have succeeded (the May 1968 events in Paris notwithstanding) in keeping class conflict latent in its decisive areas; in extending the business cycle and transforming periodic phases of capital devaluation into a permanent inflationary crisis with milder business fluctuations; and in broadly filtering the dysfunctional secondary effects of the averted economic crisis and scattering them over quasi-groups (such as consumers, schoolchildren and their parents, transportation users, the sick, the elderly, etc.) or over natural groups with little organization. In this way the social identity of classes breaks down and class consciousness is fragmented. The class compromise that has become part of the structure of advanced capitalism makes (almost) everyone at the same time both a participant and a victim. Of course, with the clearly (and increasingly) unequal distribution of wealth and power, it is important to distinguish between those belonging more to one than the other category.

The question whether, and if so how, the class structure and the principle of organization that developed in liberal capitalism have been altered through class compromise cannot be examined from the point of view of what role the principle of scarcity and the mechanism of money play at the level of the social system.[16] For the monetization of landed property and of labor, and the "progressive monetization of use values and areas of life that were heretofore closed off to the money form," do not indicate conclusively that exchange has remained the dominant medium of control over social relations.[17] Politically advanced claims to use values shed the commodity form, even if they are met with monetary rewards. What is decisive for class structure is whether the real income of the dependent worker is still based on an exchange relation, or whether production and appropriation of surplus value are limited and modified by relations of political power instead of depending on the market mechanism alone.

A theory of advanced capitalism must attempt to clarify the following questions. First:

—do the structures of advanced capitalism provide space for an evolutionary self-transformation [*Selbstaufhebung*] of the contradiction of socialized production for non-generalizable goals?
—if so, what developmental dynamic leads in this direction?
—if not, in what crisis tendencies does the temporarily suppressed, but unresolved class antagonism express itself?

Then:

> —do the structures of advanced capitalism suffice to ward off economic crisis permanently?
> —if not, does economic crisis lead, as Marx expected, through social crisis to political crisis; in other words, can there be a revolutionary struggle on a world scale?
> —if not, whither is economic crisis displaced?

Finally:

> —does the displaced crisis retain the form of a system crisis, or must we reckon with different crisis tendencies that work together?
> —if the latter is the case, which crisis tendencies are transformed into deviant behavior, and in which social groups?
> —does the expected anomic potential permit directed political action, or does it lead rather to undirected dysfunctionalization of subsystems?

At the moment I can see no possibility of cogently deciding the question about the chances for a self-transformation of advanced capitalism. But I do not exclude the possibility that economic crisis can be permanently averted, although only in such a way that contradictory steering imperatives that assert themselves in the pressure for capital realization would produce a series of other crisis tendencies. The continuing tendency toward disturbance of capitalist growth can be administratively processed and transferred, by stages, through the political and into the socio-cultural system. I am of the opinion that the contradiction of socialized production for particular ends thereby directly takes on again a political form— naturally not that of political class warfare. Because in advanced capitalism politics takes place on the basis of a processed and repressed system crisis, there are constant disputes (among shifting coalitions and with fragmented class consciousness) that can alter the terms of class compromise. Thus, whether, and to what extent, the class structure is softened and the contradiction grounded in the capitalist principle of organization itself is affected, depends on the actual constellations of power.

I shall draw up next an abstract classification of the crisis tendencies that are *possible* in advanced capitalism.

Chapter 2. Problems Resulting from Advanced-Capitalist Growth

The rapid growth processes of advanced-capitalist societies have confronted world society with problems that cannot be regarded as crisis phenomena specific to the system, although the possibilities of dealing with these crises are specifically limited by the system. I am thinking here of disturbance to ecological balance, violation of the consistency requirements of the personality system (alienation), and potentially explosive strains on international relations. With growing complexity, the system of world society shifts its boundaries so far into its environment that it runs up against limits of outer as well as inner nature. Ecological balance designates an absolute limit to growth. The less palpable anthropological balance designates another limit, which can be overstepped only at the price of altering the socio-cultural identity of social systems. The self-destructive dangers in international relations, lastly, results from the growth of forces of production that can be used destructively.

The Ecological Balance. If economic growth, in the abstract, is the result of technically informed employment of energy resources to increase the productivity of human labor, then the capitalist social formation is distinguished by its impressive solution to the problem of economic growth. Of course, with capital accumulation, economic growth is institutionalized in an unplanned, nature-like way, so that no option for self-conscious control of this process exists. Growth imperatives originally followed by capitalism have meanwhile achieved global validity through system competition and worldwide diffusion (notwithstanding stagnation or even retrogressive tendencies in some Third World countries).[1]

The established mechanisms of growth are forcing an increase in both population and production on a worldwide scale. The economic needs for a growing population and increasing productive exploitation of nature are faced with two important material limitations: on the one hand, the supply of finite resources—the area of cultivable and inhabitable land, fresh water, foodstuffs, and non-regenerating raw materials (minerals, fuels, etc.); on the other, the capacities of irreplaceable ecological systems to absorb pollutants such as radioactive by-products, carbon dioxide, or waste heat. To be sure, estimates of Forrester and others[2] on the limits of the exponential growth of population, industrial production, exploitation of natural resources, and environmental pollution have quite weak empirical foundations. The mechanisms of population growth are as little known as the outer limits of the earth's capacity to absorb even the most important pollutants. Moreover, we cannot predict technological development accurately enough to know which raw materials can be technically replaced or renewed in the future.

Even on optimistic assumptions, however, *one* absolute limitation on growth can be stated (if not, for the time being, precisely determined): namely, the limit of the environment's ability to absorb heat from energy consumption.[3] If economic growth is necessarily coupled to increasing consumption of energy, and if all natural energy that is transformed into economically useful energy is ultimately released as heat (this applies to the total energy content and not merely to that portion lost in conveyance and transformation), then the increasing consumption of energy must result, in the long run, in a rise in global temperature. Again, it is not easy to determine the critical time period empirically, since we must determine energy consumption in connection with economic growth and the influence of that consumption on the climate. (According to the present state of knowledge the critical interval is about 75–150 years.) Nevertheless, these reflections show that an exponential growth of population and production—that is, the expansion of control over outer nature—must some day run up against the limits of the biological capacity of the environment.

This limitation holds true for all complex social systems. The possible means of averting ecological crises are, in contrast, specific to systems. Capitalist societies cannot follow imperatives of growth limitation without abandoning their principle of organization; a shift from unplanned, nature-like capitalist growth to qualitative growth would require that production be planned in terms of *use*

CRISIS TENDENCIES IN ADVANCED CAPITALISM   43

values. The development of productive forces, cannot, however, be uncoupled from the production of *exchange values* without violating the logic of the system.

The Anthropological Balance. In contrast to the process of socializing outer nature, the integration of inner nature does not run up against absolute barriers. While disturbance to ecological balance indicates the degree of exploitation of natural resources, there are no clear delineations of the limits of personality systems. I doubt whether it is possible to identify any psychological constants of human nature that limit the socializing process from within. I do, however, see a limitation in the kind of socialization through which social systems have until now produced their motivations for action. The process of socialization takes place within structures of linguistic intersubjectivity; it determines an organization of behavior tied to norms requiring justification and to interpretive systems that secure identity. This communicative organization of behavior can become an obstacle to complex decisionmaking systems. As in individual organizations, steering capacity at the level of social systems presumably increases as decisionmaking authorities become functionally independent of the motivations of the members. In systems with high intrinsic complexity, the choice and realization of organization goals have to be rendered independent of the influx of narrowly circumscribed motives. This is accomplished by procuring a generalized readiness to consent, which in political systems has the form of mass loyalty. As long as we have to do with a form of socialization that binds inner nature in a communicative organization of behavior, it is inconceivable that there should be legitimation of any action norm that, even approximately, guarantees an acceptance of decisions without reasons. The motive for readiness to conform to a decisionmaking power still indeterminate in content is the expectation that this power will be exercised in accord with legitimate norms of action. The ultimate motive for readiness to follow is the citizen's conviction that he could be discursively convinced in case of doubt.[4]

These limits, fixed by the need for the legitimation of norms and by the dependence of the citizens' motives on convincing interpretations, could be broken through only if the procuring of legitimation were detached from a communicative structure of action. The form of socialization, and with it the identity of socio-cultural systems, would then have to change. Only if motives for action no longer operated through norms requiring justification, and if personality systems no longer had to find their unity in identity-securing interpretive systems, could the acceptance of decisions without reasons become routine, that is, could the readiness to conform absolutely be produced to any desired degree.[5] (I shall come back, in Part III, to the question of whether the degree of internal complexity now attained in advanced-capitalist societies is already forcing the dissolution of the communicative organization of behavior.)

The International Balance. The danger of the self-destruction of the world system through the use of thermonuclear means is on a different level. The accumulated potential for annihilation is a result of the high state of development of productive forces that, because of their technically neutral foundations, can also assume the form of destructive forces. (This has actually happened as a result of unplanned, nature-like development of international commerce.) In military action systems, parties objectify one another under the aspect of outer nature; in the organized fight to the death physical annihilation of the adversary is the *ultima ratio*. Today, for the first time, these systems have at their disposal a technical potential that can bring mortal injury to not only the adversary but also to the natural substratum of world society within reach. Consequently, international commerce is subject to a historically new imperative of self-limitation.[6] This is true for all highly militarized social systems, but, once again, the possibilities of working out these problems have limits specific to the system. If one considers the driving forces behind capitalist and post-capitalist class societies, real disarmament seems, to be sure, improbable. Yet, regulation of the arms race is not in itself incompatible with the structure of advanced-capitalist societies, at least to the extent that the system could succeed in balancing the effect of decreased government demand for unproductive goods with an increase in the use value of capital.

Chapter 3. A Classification of Possible Crisis Tendencies

We shall leave aside the global dangers that are *consequences of capitalist growth* and limit ourselves to *crisis tendencies specific to the system.* Crises can arise at different points; and the forms in which a crisis tendency manifests itself up to the point of its political eruption—that is, the point at which the existing political system is delegitimized—are just as diverse. I see four *possible* crisis tendencies, which are listed in the following table.

Point of Origin	System Crisis	Identity Crisis
Economic System	Economic Crisis	——
Political System	Rationality Crisis	Legitimation Crisis
Socio-Cultural System	——	Motivation Crisis

Economic Crisis Tendencies. The economic system requires an input of work and capital. The output consists in consumable values, which are distributed over time according to quantity and type among social strata. A crisis that derives from inadequate input is atypical of the capitalist mode of production. The disturbances of liberal capitalism were output crises. The crisis cycle again and again placed in question the distribution of values in conformity with the system. ("In conformity with the system" here means all patterns of distribution of burdens and rewards permissible within the range of variation of the legitimating value system.) If economic crisis tendencies persist in advanced capitalism, this indicates that government actions intervening in the realization process obey, no less than exchange processes, spontaneously working economic laws. Consequently, they are subject to the logic of the economic crisis as expressed in the law of the tendential fall of the rate of profit. According to this thesis, the state pursues the continuation of the politics of capital by other means.[1] The altered forms of appearance (such as crises in government finances, permanent inflation, growing disparities between public poverty and private wealth, etc.) are explained by the fact that self-regulation of the realization process now also operates through legitimate power as a medium of control. But since the crisis tendency is still determined by the law of value—that is, the structurally necessary asymmetry in the exchange of wage labor for capital—the activity of the state cannot compensate for the tendency of the falling rate of profit. It can at best mediate it, that is, itself consummate it by political means. Thus, economic crisis tendency will also assert itself as a social crisis and lead to political struggles in which class opposition between owners of capital and masses dependent on wages again becomes manifest. According to another version, the state apparatus does not obey the logic of the law of value in an unplanned, nature-like manner, but consciously looks after the interests of united monopoly capitalists. This agency theory, tailored to advanced capitalism, conceives of the state, not as a blind organ of the realization process, but as a potent collective capitalist [*Gesamtkapitalist*] who makes the accumulation of capital the substance of political planning.

Political Crisis Tendencies. The political system requires an input of mass loyalty that is as diffuse as possible. The output consists in sovereignly executed administrative decisions. Output crises have the form of a *rationality crisis* in which the administrative system does not succeed in reconciling and fulfilling the imperatives received from the economic system. Input crises have the form of a *legitimation crisis*; the legitimizing system does not succeed in maintaining the requisite level of mass loyalty while the steering imperatives taken over from the economic system are carried through. Although both crisis tendencies arise in the political system, they differ in their form of appearance. The rationality crisis is a displaced systemic crisis which, like economic crisis, expresses the contradiction between socialized production for non-generalizable interests and steering imperatives. This crisis tendency is converted into the withdrawal of legitimation by way of a disorganization of the state apparatus. The legitimation crisis, by contrast, is directly an identity crisis. It does not proceed by way of endangering system integration, but results from the fact that the fulfillment of governmental planning tasks places in question the structure of the depoliticized public realm and, thereby, the formally democratic securing of the private autonomous disposition of the means of production.

We can speak of a rationality crisis in the strict sense only if it takes the place of economic crisis. In this case, the logic of problems of capital realization is not merely reflected in another steering medium, that of legitimate power; rather, the crisis logic is itself altered by the displacement of the contradictory steering imperatives from market commerce into the administrative system. This assertion is advanced in two versions. One version starts with the familiar thesis of the anarchy of commodity production that is built into market commerce.[2] On the one hand, in advanced capitalism the need for administrative planning to secure the realization of capital grows. On the other hand, the private autonomous disposition of the means of production demands a limitation to state intervention and prohibits planned coordination of the contradictory interests of individual capitalists. Another version has been developed by Offe.[3] While the state compensates for the weaknesses of a self-blocking economic system and takes over tasks complementary to the market, it is forced by the logic of its means of control to admit more and more foreign elements into the system. The problems of an economic system controlled by imperatives of capital realization cannot be taken over into the administratively controlled domain, and processed there, without the spread of orientations alien to the structure.

A rationality deficit in public administration means that the state apparatus cannot, under given boundary conditions, adequately steer the economic system. A legitimation deficit means that it is not possible by administrative means to maintain or establish effective normative structures to the extent required. During the course of capitalist development, the political system shifts its boundaries not only into the economic system but also into the socio-cultural system. While organizational rationality spreads, cultural traditions are undermined and weakened. The residue of tradition must, however, escape the administrative grasp, for traditions important for legitimation cannot be regenerated administratively. Furthermore, administrative manipulation of cultural matters has the unintended side effect of causing meanings and norms previously fixed by tradition and belonging to the *boundary* conditions of the political system to be publicly thematized. In this way, the scope of discursive will-formation expands—a process that

shakes the structures of the depoliticized public realm so important
for the continued existence of the system.

Socio-Cultural Crisis Tendencies. The socio-cultural system receives
its input from the economic and political systems in the form of
purchasable and collectively demandable goods and services, legal
and administrative acts, public and social security, etc. Output
crises in both of the other systems are also input disturbances in the
socio-cultural system and translate into withdrawal of legitimation.
The aforementioned crisis tendencies can break out only through
the socio-cultural system. For the social integration of a society is
dependent on the output of this system—directly on the motivations it supplies to the political system in the form of legitimation
and indirectly on the motivations to perform it supplies to the
educational and occupational systems. Since the socio-cultural
system does not, in contrast to the economic system, organize its
own input, there can be no socio-culturally produced input crisis.
Crises that arise at this point are always output crises. We have to
reckon with cultural crisis tendencies when the normative structures change, according to their inherent logic, in such a way that
the complementarity between the requirements of the state
apparatus and the occupational system, on the one hand, and the
interpreted needs and legitimate expectations of members of
society, on the other, is disturbed. Legitimation crises result from a
need for legitimation that arises from changes in the political
system (even when normative structures remain unchanged) and
that cannot be met by the existing supply of legitimation. Motivational crises, on the other hand, are a result of changes in the
socio-cultural system itself.

In advanced capitalism such tendencies are becoming apparent
at the level of cultural tradition (moral systems, world-views) as
well as at the level of structural change in the system of
childrearing (school and family, mass media). In this way, the
residue of tradition off which the state and the system of social
labor lived in liberal capitalism is eaten away (stripping away
traditionalistic padding), and core components of the bourgeois
ideology become questionable (endangering civil and familial-pro-

fessional privatism). On the other hand, the remains of bourgeois ideologies (belief in science, post-auratic art, and universalistic value systems) form a normative framework that is dysfunctional. Advanced capitalism creates "new" needs it cannot satisfy.[4]

Our abstract survey of *possible* crisis tendencies in advanced capitalism has served an analytic purpose. I maintain that advanced-capitalist societies, assuming that they have not altogether overcome the susceptibility to crisis intrinsic to capitalism, are in danger from at least one of these possible crisis tendencies. It is a consequence of the fundamental contradiction of the capitalist system that, other factors being equal, either

- —the economic system does not produce the requisite quantity of consumable values, or;
- —the administrative system does not produce the requisite quantity of rational decisions, or;
- —the legitimation system does not provide the requisite quantity of generalized motivations, or;
- —the socio-cultural system does not generate the requisite quantity of action-motivating meaning.

The expression "the requisite quantity" refers to the extent, quality, and temporal dimension of the respective system performances (value, administrative decision, legitimation and meaning). Substitution relations between different system performances themselves are not excluded. Whether performances of the subsystems can be adequately operationalized and isolated and the critical need for system performances adequately specified is another question. This task may be difficult to solve for pragmatic reasons. But it is insoluble, in principle, only if levels of development of a social system—and in this way identity-guaranteeing limits of variation of its goal states—cannot be determined within the framework of a theory of social evolution.[5]

Of course, the same macrophenomena may be an expression of different crisis tendencies. Each individual crisis argument, if it proves correct, is a sufficient explanation of a possible case of crisis. But in the explanation of actual cases of crisis, several arguments can supplement one another. I assert analytical completeness only for the crisis tendencies and not, of course, for the list of explanatory arguments, which I would like to discuss briefly below.

Crisis Tendencies	Proposed Explanations
Economic Crisis	*a)* the state apparatus acts as unconscious, nature-like executive organ of the law of value;
	b) the state apparatus acts as planning agent of united "monopoly capital."
Rationality Crisis	destruction of administrative rationality occurs through
	c) opposed interests of individual capitalists;
	d) the production (necessary for continued existence) of structures foreign to the system.
Legitimation Crisis	*e)* systematic limits;
	f) unintended side effects (politicization) of administrative interventions in the cultural tradition;
Motivation Crisis	*g)* erosion of traditions important for continued existence;
	h) overloading through universalistic value-systems ("new" needs).

Chapter 4. Theorems of Economic Crisis

Even in liberal capitalism the market did not assume the functions of social integration alone. The class relationship could assume the unpolitical form of the relation of wage labor to capital only when the general prerequisites for the continued existence of capitalist production were fulfilled by the state. Only state functions that supplement, but are not subject to, the market mechanism make possible unpolitical domination through private appropriation of socially produced surplus value. Capital formation takes place in a situation of unlimited competition. However, the supporting conditions of this competition—the social foundations of the production of surplus value—cannot themselves be reproduced by capitalist means. They require a state that confronts individual capitalists as a non-capitalist in order to carry through vicariously the "collective-capitalist will" absent in the competitive sphere. With respect to its non-capitalist means, the state *limits* capitalist production; with respect to its function, it *serves* to maintain it in existence. Only insofar as the state *supplements* the economy can it be *instrumental* for it.[1]

This conception has also been applied to the state apparatus in advanced capitalism.[2] According to this thesis, of course, the state cannot limit itself today to fulfilling general conditions of production. It must also intervene in the reproduction process itself—that is, it must create conditions for utilizing fallow capital, improve the use value of capital, curb externalized costs and consequences of capitalist production, adjust disproportionalities that restrict growth, regulate the overall economic cycle through social, tax, and business policies, etc. But state interventions are nonetheless actions, although instrumental for capital realization, of a non-capitalist who vicariously asserts the collective-capitalist will.

According to *the orthodox position*, the advanced-capitalist state remains an "ideal collective capitalist" (Engels) insofar as it in no way suspends the nature-like development of anarchical commodity production. It limits capitalist production but does not control it like a collective-capitalist planning authority. In contrast to the liberal-capitalist state, the interventionist state is, to be sure, implicated in the process of reproduction. It not only secures the general conditions of production, but itself becomes a kind of executive organ of the law of value. Government activity does not suspend the spontaneous working of the law of value but is rather subject to it. Hence, in the long run, administrative activity must even intensify economic crisis.[3] Even the class struggle, which can lead to legal regulations in the interest of wage labor (as Marx showed in his example of contemporary legislation for the protection of labor), remains a "moment of the movement of capital."[4]

In this view, the substitution of governmental functions for market functions does not in fact alter the unconscious character of the overall economic process, as can be seen in the strict limitations imposed on state manipulation. The state cannot intervene substantially in the property structure without setting off an "investment strike"; nor can it avoid, in the long run, cyclical disturbances of the accumulation process, that is, endogenously produced stagnation tendencies; nor can it even control crisis substitutes, that is, chronic deficits in the public budget and inflation.

The *general objection* to this view is that the question, whether—and if so how—the class structure has changed, can be answered only empirically. It cannot be determined in advance at the analytic level. Absolutizing the conceptual strategy of value theory deprives the economic theory of crisis of a possible empirical test. Even Marx could only ground his claim to have grasped the crisis-ridden pattern of development of the social system as a whole (including political disputes and the functions of the state apparatus) by means of an economic analysis of the laws of motion of capital formation, by pointing out that the exercise of class domination had assumed the unpolitical form of the exchange of wage labor for capital. However, this improbable constellation has changed, and socially integrative functions of maintaining legitimacy can no longer be fulfilled through system-integrative functions of the market and decrepit remains of pre-capitalist traditions. They must again pass over into the political system. Government activity now pursues the declared goal of steering the system so as to avoid crises, and, consequently, the class relationship has lost its unpolitical form. For these reasons, class structure *must* be maintained in struggles over the administratively mediated distribution of increases in the social product. Thus the class structure can now be directly affected by political disputes as well. Under these conditions, economic processes can no longer be conceived immanently as movements of a self-regulating economic system. The law of value can express the double character of exchange processes (as steering processes and exploitation) only when conditions, approximately met in liberal capitalism, allow class domination to be exercised unpolitically. How, and to what extent, power is exercised and exploitation secured through economic processes depends today on concrete power constellations that are no longer *predetermined* by an autonomously effective mechanism of the labor market. Today the state has to fulfill functions that can be neither explained with reference to prerequisites of the continued existence of the mode of production, nor derived from the immanent movement of capital. This movement is no longer realized through a market mechanism that can be comprehended in the theory of value, but is a result of the still effective economic driving forces and a political countercontrol in which *a displacement of the relations of production* finds expression.

In order to be able to grasp this displacement more precisely, it is meaningful to distinguish four categories of governmental activity as it relates to imperatives of the economic system.

—In order to *constitute* the mode of production and to maintain it, the prerequisites of continued existence must be realized. The state secures the system of civil law with the core institutions of property and of freedom of contract; it protects the market system from self-destructive side effects (for example, through introduction of the normal working day, anti-trust legislation, and stabilization of the currency); it fulfills the prerequisites of production in the economy as a whole (such as education, transportation, and communication); it promotes the capability of the domestic economy for international competition (for example, through trade and tariff policies); and it reproduces itself through military preservation of national integrity abroad and paramilitary suppression of enemies of the system at home.

—The accumulation process of capital requires adaptation of the legal system to new forms of business organization, competition, financing, etc. (for example, through creating new legal arrangements in banking and business law and manipulating the tax system). In doing so the state limits itself to *market-complementing* adaptations to a process whose dynamic it does not influence. Thus the social principle of organization, as well as the class structure, remain unaffected.

—These actions are to be distinguished from the *market-replacing* actions of the state. The latter do not simply take into account legally economic states of affairs that have arisen independently but, *in reaction to the weaknesses of the economic driving forces*, make possible the continuance of an accumulation process no longer left to its own dynamic. Such actions thereby create new economic states of affairs, whether through creating and improving chances

for investment (governmental demand for unproductive
commodities) or through altered forms of production of
surplus value (governmental organization of scientific-technical progress, occupational qualification of labor forces,
etc.). In both cases, the principle of organization is affected,
as can be seen in the rise of a public sector foreign to the
system.

—Finally, the state *compensates* for dysfunctional consequences of the accumulation process that have elicited
politically effective reactions on the part of individual
capital groupings, organized labor, or other organized
groups. Thus, on the one hand, the state takes charge of the
externalized consequences of private enterprise (for example, ecological damage) or it secures the survival capacity of
endangered sectors (for example, mining and agriculture)
through structural policy measures. On the other hand, it
enacts regulations and interventions demanded by unions
and reformist parties with the aim of improving the social
situation of the dependent workers. (Historically such
interventions begin with the right of labor to organize and
extend through improvements in wages, working conditions,
and social welfare to educational, health, and transportation
policies.) The beginnings of the state expenditures classified
today as "social expenses" and "social consumption" [5] can
be traced back, in large part, to politically achieved
demands of organized labor.[6]

Governmental activity in the last two categories is typical of
organized capitalism. The proposed analytical distinction is difficult
to draw empirically in many cases because the advanced-capitalist
state manages the tasks in the first two categories as well. And it
does so to a considerably greater extent and, naturally, with the
same techniques employed in managing tasks that have recently
accrued to it. Thus, monetary policy is today an essential part of a
state's global planning, although the securing of international
commerce in currency and capital, and the reaction to it, belong to
the actions that constitute the mode of production. The criteria of
demarcation are not the extent and the technique of governmental

activity, but its functions. The liberal-capitalist state takes action, if our model is correct, in order to secure the prerequisites for the continued existence of the mode of production and—as a supplement to the market mechanism—to satisfy the needs of the accumulation process controlled by the market. To be sure, the advanced-capitalist state also does precisely this, to an even greater extent and with more efficient techniques. But it can fulfill these tasks only, and only insofar as, it simultaneously fills functional gaps in the market, intervenes in the process of accumulation, and compensates for its politically intolerable consequences. In actions of this kind, reaction formations to the changes in class structure—that is, *other* constellations of power—are realized. As a consequence, the principle of societal organization, which rests ultimately on the institutionalization of an unorganized labor market, is also affected.

Three developments, above all, are characteristic of the change in the relations of production in advanced capitalism: (*a*) an altered form of the production of surplus value, which affects the principle of societal organization; (*b*) a quasi-political wage structure, which expresses a class compromise; and (*c*) the growing need for legitimation of the political system, which brings into play demands oriented to use values (demands that in certain circumstances are in competition with the needs of capital realization).

Re: *a*) The rise of a public sector is, among other things, an indication that the state looks after the production of collective commodities, which it makes available at a saving for private use in the form of the material and immaterial infrastructure.[7] In performing this function, the state improves the use value of individual capitals, for collective commodities serve to heighten the productivity of labor. In terms of the theory of value, this fact is expressed in the cheapening of constant capital and a rise in the rate of surplus value.[8] Governmental organization of the educational system, which raises the productivity of human labor through qualification, has the same effect.[9] These governmental functions alter the form of production of surplus value.[10] After the raising of *absolute* surplus value through physical force, lengthening the working day, recruiting underpaid labor forces (women, children), etc. had run up against natural boundaries (even in liberal capitalism, as the introduction of a normal working day shows), the raising of *relative* surplus value first took the form of utilizing *existing or externally generated* inventions and information for the development of the technical and human forces of production. Only with governmental organization of scientific-technical progress and a systematically managed expansion of the system of continuing education does the production of information, technologies, organizations, and qualifications that heighten productivity become a component of the production process itself. Reflexive labor, that is, labor applied to itself with the aim of increasing the productivity of labor, could be regarded at first as a collective natural commodity. Today it is internalized in the economic cycle. For the state (or private enterprise) now expends capital to purchase the *indirectly productive* labor power of scientists, engineers, teachers, etc. and to transform the products of their labor into cost-cutting commodities of the category referred to.[11] If one holds fast to a dogmatic conceptual strategy and conceives of reflexive labor as unproductive labor (in the Marxian sense), the specific function of this labor for the realization process is overlooked. Reflexive labor is not productive in the sense of the direct production of surplus value. But it is also not unproductive; for then it would have no net effect on the production of surplus value. Marx saw precisely "that, even with a given magnitude of functioning capital, the labor power, the science, and the land (by which are to be understood, economically, all conditions of labor furnished by Nature independently of man), embodied in it, form *elastic powers* of capital, allowing it, within certain limits, a field of action independent of its own magnitude."[12] But he was able to treat "science," like "land," as a free collective commodity without having to consider the reflexive labor expended in its production as a peculiar factor of production. The variable capital that is paid out as income for reflexive labor is indirectly productively invested, as it systematically alters conditions under which surplus value can be appropriated from productive labor. Thus, it indirectly contributes to production of more surplus value. This reflection shows, firstly, that the classical fundamental categories of the theory of value are insufficient for the analysis of governmental policy in education, technology, and science. It also shows that it is an empirical question whether the new form of production of surplus value can compensate for the tendential fall in the rate of profit, that is, whether it can work against economic crisis.[13]

Re: *b*) In the monopolistic sector, by means of a coalition between business associations and unions, the price of the commodity known as labor power is quasi-politically negotiated. In these "labor markets" the mechanism of competition is replaced by the compromises between organizations to which the state has delegated legitimate power. This erosion of the mechanism of the labor market has, of course, economic consequences (such as shifting the increase in factor-costs to the price of the product). But these are really consequences of the suspension of an unpolitical class relationship. Through the system of "political" [14] wages, negotiated on the basis of wage scales, it has been possible—above all in the capital- and growth-intensive sectors of the economy—to mitigate the opposition between wage labor and capital and to bring about a partial class compromise. From a Marxian point of view, it is also possible, in principle, to analyze price setting in organized markets, within the framework of the theory of value—a good can be sold above its value. But here the price of the commodity labor power is the unit of measure in the value calculation. Quasi-political price setting in the labor market cannot, therefore, be treated in an analogous way. For it determines, in turn, through the average wage level, the quantity of value against which deviations of labor power sold above value must be measured. We know of no standard for the costs of the reproduction of labor power that is independent of cultural norms; nor does Marx start from such a standard.[15] Of course, one can again hold fast to a dogmatic conceptual strategy and equate by definition the average wage with the costs of the reproduction of labor power. But in so doing one prejudices at the analytical level the (no doubt) empirically substantial question of whether the class struggle, organized politically and through unionization, has perhaps had a stabilizing effect only because it has been successful in an economic sense and has visibly altered the rate of exploitation to the advantage of the best organized parts of the working class.

Re: *c*) Finally, the relations of production are altered because the replacement of exchange relations by administrative power is linked to a condition in which legitimate power must be available for administrative planning. Functions that have accrued to the state apparatus in advanced capitalism and extension of administratively processed social matters increase the need for legitimation. There is no question here of some mysterious magnitude; the need for legitimation arises from evident functional conditions of an administrative system that steps into functional gaps in the market. Considering the context of bourgeois revolutions, it is understandable that liberal capitalism was constituted in the form of bourgeois democracy. Because it was, the growing need for legitimation must be satisfied by means of political democracy (based on universal suffrage). Once again, a dogmatic conceptual strategy, which admits bourgeois democracy only as a superstructure of capitalist class domination, misses the specific problem. To the extent that the state no longer represents merely the superstructure of an unpolitical class relationship, the formally democratic means for procuring legitimation prove to be peculiarly restrictive. That is, in these circumstances, the administrative system is forced to meet use value-oriented demands with available means of control. As long as the capitalist economic system begot of itself a viable ideology, a comparable legitimation problem (which sets restrictive conditions to the solution of the problem of capital realization) could not arise.

New legitimation problems cannot be subsumed under a too generalized imperative of self-maintenance, as they cannot be solved without regard to the satisfaction of legitimate needs—that is, to the distribution of use values—while the interests of capital realization prohibit precisely this consideration. Legitimation problems cannot be reduced to problems of capital realization. Because a class compromise has been made the foundation of reproduction, the state apparatus must fulfill its tasks in the economic system under the limiting condition that mass loyalty be simultaneously secured within the framework of a formal democracy and in accord with ruling universalistic value systems. These pressures of legitimation can be mitigated only through structures of a depoliticized public realm. A structurally secured civil privatism becomes necessary for continued existence because there are no functional equivalents for it. Hence, there arises a new level of susceptibility to crisis that cannot be grasped from the orthodox position.

A *revisionist version* is contained in the economic crisis theory of leading economists of the German Democratic Republic. The theory of state-monopolistic capitalism[16] is not subject to the aforementioned objections because it proceeds from the assumption that the unplanned, nature-like development of the capitalist process of reproduction has been replaced by state-monopolistic planning; the spontaneous working of economic laws is replaced by centralized steering of the production apparatus. The high degree to which production is socialized brings about a convergence between individual interests of large corporations and the collective-capitalist interest in maintaining the system. This convergence develops furthermore as the continued existence of the system is threatened externally by competing post-capitalist societies and internally by forces that transcend the system. Thus, a collective-capitalist interest takes shape, which the united monopolies consciously pursue with the aid of the state apparatus. To this new stage of consciousness there supposedly corresponds a capitalist planning that guarantees the production of surplus value in such a way that it partially frees investment decisions from the market mechanism. The alleged union of the power of the monopolies with that of the state apparatus is described in terms of an agency theory. The societal control center is allegedly subordinated to the collective-capitalist interest in the sense that a (in itself progressive) form of organization for controlling production remains tied to the goal of capital realization. The open repoliticizing of the class relationship, on the other hand, renders state-monopolistic rule susceptible to political pressures that democratic forces (in the form of a popular front) can exercise. The theory of state-monopolistic capitalism also begins with the principle that the fundamental contradiction of capitalist production is not averted but is sharpened in the new form of organization. However, the economic crisis now takes on a directly political form.

Two objections have been made to this theory.[17] First, the assumption that the state apparatus can actively plan, put forward, and carry through a central economic strategy, in whoever's interest, cannot be empirically verified. The theory of state-monopolistic capitalism fails to appreciate (as do Western technocratic theories) the limits of administrative planning in advanced capitalism. The form of motion of planning bureaucracies is reactive avoidance of crisis. The various bureaucracies are, moreover, incompletely coordinated and, because of their deficient capacity for perceiving and planning, dependent on the influence of their clients.[18] It is precisely this deficient rationality of governmental administration that guarantees the success of organized special interests. Contradictions among the interests of individual capitalists, between individual interests and the collective-capitalist interest, and finally, between interests specific to the system and generalizable interests, are displaced into the state apparatus.

Second, the assumption that the state acts as the agent of the united monopolists cannot be supported empirically. The theory of state-monopolistic capitalism overestimates (in the same way as Western elitist theories do) the significance of personal contacts and direct regulation of transactions. Investigations into the recruitment, composition, and interaction of various power elites cannot adequately explain the functional connections between economic and administrative systems.[19] The systems-theoretic model developed by Offe and his collaborators seems to me more suitable. It distinguishes between the structure of an administrative system, on the one hand, and the processes of conflict resolution and consensus formation, of decision and implementation, on the other. In doing so, Offe conceives "structure" as a set of sedimented selection rules that prejudice what is recognized as a matter requiring regulation, what is thematized, what—with what priority and by which means—is actually publicly regulated, etc. The relatively stable administrative patterns of helping and hindering are objectively functional for capital realization, that is, they are independent of the professed intentions of the administration. They can be explained with the aid of selection rules that predetermine the consideration or suppression of problems, themes, arguments, and interests.[20]

Chapter 5. Theorems of Rationality Crisis

The mode of functioning of the advanced-capitalist state can be adequately conceived neither through the model of an unconsciously acting executive organ of economic laws that are still spontaneously effective, nor through the model of an agent of the united monopoly capitalists that acts according to plan. Involved as it is in the production process, the state has altered the determinants of the realization process itself. On the basis of a class compromise, the administrative system gains a limited planning capacity, which can be used, within the framework of a formally democratic procurement of legitimation, for purposes of reactive crisis avoidance. In this situation, the collective-capitalist interest in system maintenance is in competition, on the one hand, with the contradictory interests of the individual capital groupings and, on the other, with the generalizable interests, oriented to use values, of various population groups. The crisis cycle, distributed over time and defused of its social consequences, is replaced by inflation and a permanent crisis in public finances. Whether this replacement phenomenon indicates a successful mastery of economic crisis or only its temporary displacement into the political system is an empirical question. In the final analysis, the answer depends on whether capital expended so as to be only indirectly productive does attain an increase in the productivity of labor, and on whether the distribution of the growth in productivity in line with functional requirements of the system is sufficient to guarantee mass loyalty and, simultaneously, keep the accumulation process moving.

The government budget is burdened with the common costs of a more-and-more-socialized production. It bears the costs of imperialistic market strategies and the costs of demand for unproductive commodities (armaments and space travel). It bears the infrastructural costs directly related to production (transportation and communication systems, scientific-technical progress, vocational training). It bears the costs of social consumption indirectly related to production (housing construction, transportation, health care, leisure, education, social security). It bears the costs of social welfare, especially unemployment. And, finally, it bears the externalized costs of environmental strain arising from private production. In the end, these expenditures have to be financed through taxes. The state apparatus is, therefore, faced simultaneously with two tasks. On the one hand, it is supposed to raise the requisite amount of taxes by skimming off profits and income and to use the available taxes so rationally that crisis-ridden disturbances of growth can be avoided. On the other hand, the selective raising of taxes, the discernible pattern of priorities in their use, and the administrative performances themselves must be so constituted that the need for legitimation can be satisfied as it arises. If the state fails in the former task, there is a deficit in administrative rationality. If it fails in the latter task, a deficit in legitimation results. (See Chapter 6, below.)

A rationality deficit can arise because contradictory steering imperatives, which cause the unplanned, nature-like development of an anarchistic commodity production and its crisis-ridden growth, are then operative within the administrative system. Evidence for this modified-anarchy thesis has been supplied by Hirsch, among others, using examples from the administration of science.[1] The thesis has a certain descriptive value, for it is possible to show that the authorities, with little informational and planning capacity and insufficient coordination among themselves, are dependent on the flow of information from their clients. They are thus unable to preserve the distance from them necessary for independent decisions. Individual sectors of the economy can, as it were, privatize parts of the public administration, thus displacing the competition between individual social interests into the state apparatus. The crisis theorem is based now on the reflection that growing socialization of production still adjusted to private ends brings with it unfulfillable—because paradoxical—demands on the state apparatus. On the one hand, the state is supposed to act as a collective capitalist. On the other hand, competing individual capitals cannot form or carry through a collective will as long as freedom of investment is not eliminated. Thus arise the mutually contradictory imperatives of expanding the planning capacity of the state with the aim of a collective-capitalist planning and, yet, blocking precisely this expansion, which would threaten the continued existence of capitalism. Thus the state apparatus vacillates between expected intervention and forced renunciation of intervention, between becoming independent of its clients in a way that threatens the system and subordinating itself to their particular interests. Rationality deficits are the unavoidable result of a snare of relations into which the advanced-capitalist state fumbles and in which its contradictory activities must become more and more muddled.[2]

I shall mention three of the objections that have been made to this argument.

a) Since the fundamental contradiction of capitalism is displaced from the economic into the administrative system, the terms in which it can possibly be resolved also change. In the economic system, contradictions are expressed directly in relations between quantities of values and indirectly in the social consequences of capital loss (bankruptcy) and deprivation of the means of subsistence (unemployment). In the administrative system, contradictions are expressed in irrational decisions and in the social consequences of administrative failure, that is, in disorganization of areas of life. Bankruptcy and unemployment mark unambiguously recognizable thresholds of risk for the non-fulfillment of functions. The disorganization of areas of life moves, in contrasts, along a continuum. And it is difficult to say where the thresholds of tolerance lie and to what extent the perception of what is still tolerated—and of what is already experienced as intolerable—can be adapted to an increasingly disorganized environment.

b) Even more important is the fact that in the economic system, the rules of strategic action, like the dimensions of gain and loss, are set. The medium of exchange does not permit conflict resolution by way of a constant, mutual adaptation of action orientations; the controlling principle of maximization of gain is not disposable. The administrative system, in contrast, enters into compromise-oriented negotiations with the sectors of society on which it depends. "Bargaining" is applied under pressure to the reciprocal adaptation of structures of expectation and value systems. The reactive manner in which avoidance strategies operate expresses the limited maneuvering capability of the state apparatus. The state *can* make visible to its negotiating partners how the generalizable interests of the population differ from organized individual interests as well as from the collective-capitalist interest in the continued existence of the system. However, the use of legitimate power requires *taking into consideration a legitimation gradient* between *different* domains of interest; but such a gradient cannot exist within an exchange system legitimated as a whole.

c) Finally, crisis tendencies cannot assert themselves through collective administrative action unconsciously in the same way as they can through the particularized behavior of individual market participants. That is, for the medium of the exercise of power, the distinction between unplanned, nature-like processes and planning is no longer sharp, as it is for strategic games in which the intentional following of rules can have unintended side effects. Instead, *crisis avoidance is thematized* as the goal of action. For the character of decision processes lying in the twilight zone between unplanned, nature-like development and development according to plan, the distinctive mode of justification is that which the administrative system and its negotiating partners follow. Demanded or desired administrative action is justified in each case by a systemic rationality projected from action perspectives,[3] that is, by functional control performances for fictive goal functions that—since none of the participants runs the system—no one can fulfill. Political compromises do not form, as do the decisions of economic choice in the market-controlled system, a nature-like context woven from purposive-rational individual actions. Thus there exists no *logically necessary* incompatibility between interests in global capitalist planning and freedom of investment, need for planning and renunciation of intervention, and independence of the state apparatus and dependency on individual interests. The possibility that the administrative system might open a compromise path between competing claims that would allow a sufficient amount of organizational rationality, cannot be excluded from the start on logical grounds.

Taking these objections into account, one can, of course, attempt to construct a second stage of unplanned, nature-like development for the administrative system. The different variants of bureaucratically independent capitalist planning[4] are also distinguishable from the type of democratic planning coupled to democratic will-formation in the quantity of unanticipated problems that result from each and that must be worked out, case by case, in an *ad hoc* manner. These problems can become so concentrated that in the end even recourse to the resource of time no longer offers a way out. The crisis theorem could be reformulated as follows: this form of *secondary unconsciousness* builds a façade behind which the state apparatus must withdraw in order to minimize the costs that arise from compensations to dispossessed victims of the accumulation process. Even today capitalist growth takes place by way of concentration of enterprises and by centralization and shifting of capital ownership,[5] which make the expropriation and redistribution of capital a normal occurrence. Precisely this normality becomes problematic to the extent that the state lays claim to the role of a responsible planning authority that those affected can burden with their losses and that they can confront with demands for compensation and prevention. The effectiveness of this mechanism is reflected, for example, in structural policy. To the extent that economic resources are not sufficient to sustain fully capitalist victims of capitalist growth, there arises the dilemma of either immunizing the state against such claims or crippling the process of growth. The first alternative leads to a new aporia. In order to guarantee the continuation of the accumulation process, the state must assume ever clearer planning functions. But these must not be recognizable as administrative performances for which the state is accountable, because it would otherwise be liable for compensations, which retard accumulation. In this form, the theorem of the rationality crisis remains, to be sure, dependent on empirical assumptions about economic bottlenecks in capitalist growth.

One must also take into account that an exponentially rising need for planning creates bottlenecks not specific to the system. Long-term planning in complex societies confronts every administrative system—not only the advanced-capitalist—with structural difficulties that F. W. Scharpf has subjected to clear-sighted analysis in several works.[6] I am inclined to assume that not *every* incrementalism—that is, every type of planning limited to middle-range horizons and sensitive to external impulses—*eo ipso* reflects the rationality deficit of an overloaded administration. One can, in any event, adduce logical grounds for the limits to the rationality of an avoidance activity that has to investigate the *compromisibility* of interests without being able beforehand to bring up for public discussion the generalizability of these interests. The advanced-capitalist limitation on rationality consists in the structural inadmissibility of that type of planning which, following R. Funke, could be designated as democratic incrementalism.[7]

Another argument for the unavoidable development of rationality deficits in administrative planning is from an original reflection of C. Offe. Offe designates three tendencies that provide evidence that propagation of elements hostile to the system is systematically inevitable. They concern the spread of patterns of orientation that make it difficult to sustain behavioral control conforming to the system.[8]

First, the boundary conditions under which strategic business decisions are made are altered in the organized markets of the public and monopoly sectors. Large corporations have such a broad temporal and material range of alternatives in which to arrive at their decisions that an investment *policy* (which requires additional premises for its foundation) takes the place of rational choice determined by external data. Higher management must therefore adopt political patterns of evaluation and decision, instead of action *strategies* fixed *a priori*.

Moreover, in connection with the functions of the public sector, there arise occupational spheres in which abstract labor is increasingly replaced by concrete labor, that is, labor oriented to use values. This is true even of those employed in the bureaucracies entrusted with planning tasks. It is true of public service sectors (transportation, health care, housing, leisure). It is true of the scientific and educational systems, and of research and technological development. *Radical professionalism* is an indication that professional work in such areas can be detached from privatistic career patterns and market mechanisms and can be oriented to concrete goals.

Finally, the inactive proportion of the population, which does not reproduce itself through the labor market, grows *vis-à-vis* the active population, which receives income. The former includes schoolchildren and students, the unemployed, those living on annuities, welfare recipients, non-professionalized housewives, the sick, and the criminal. These groups too may develop orientation patterns like those that arise in contexts of concrete labor.

These "foreign bodies" in the capitalist employment system proliferate to the extent that production is socialized; and they have a restrictive effect on administrative planning. Taking into consideration the investment freedom of private enterprise, capitalist planning makes use of global steering, which influences its addressees through altering external facts. The parameters it can alter in conformity with the system—namely, interest rates, taxes, subsidies, business commissions, secondary distribution of income, etc.—are as a rule monetary values. It is precisely these values that lose their steering effect as abstract orientations to exchange value become weaker. The problematic consequences of a socialization of production, speeded up through state intervention, therefore destroy the conditions for application of important instruments of state intervention itself. This argument does not, of course, have the force of a logical contradiction.

The three aforementioned tendencies support the view that the process of accumulation takes place through media other than that of exchange. However, the political quality the once-market-rational decisions now take on, the politicization of certain occupational orientations, and the socialization—unconnected with the market—of those who do not receive income, do not, *per se*, have to narrow the maneuvering space of the administration. Even participation can, with certain precautions, be more functional for the carrying through of administrative planning than behavioral reactions controlled by external stimuli.[9] *To the extent* that these developments actually lead to crisis-related bottlenecks, it is a question, not of deficits in planning rationality, but of consequences of unadapted motivational situations. The administration is not able to motivate its partners to cooperate. Roughly speaking, advanced capitalism need not suffer damages when the means of control through external stimulation fail in certain behavioral spheres in which they previously functioned. But it does fall into difficulties when the administrative system can no longer take on planning functions important for continued existence because control, by whatever means, over planning-related areas of behavior, has in general slipped from its grasp. But this prediction cannot be inferred from a withering of rationality in administration but, at best, from a withering of motivations necessary to the system. (See Chapter 7 below.)

Chapter 6.   *Theorems of Legitimation Crisis*

The concept of the rationality crisis is modeled after that of the economic crisis. According to that concept, contradictory steering imperatives assert themselves through the purposive-rational actions not of market-participants but of members of the administration; they manifest themselves in contradictions that directly threaten system integration and thus endanger social integration.

We have seen that an economic system crisis can be counted on only as long as political disputes (class struggles) maintain and do not change institutional boundary conditions of capitalist production (for example, the Chartist movement and introduction of the normal working day). To the extent that the class relationship has itself been repoliticized and the state has taken over market-replacing as well as market-supplementing tasks (and made possible a "more elastic" form of production of surplus value), class domination can no longer take the anonymous form of the law of value. Instead, it now depends on factual constellations of power whether, and how, production of surplus value can be guaranteed through the public sector, and how the terms of the class compromise look. With this development, crisis tendencies shift, of course, from the economic into the administrative system. Indeed, the self-containment of exchange processes, mediated only through the market, is destroyed. But after the liberal-capitalist spell of commodity production is broken (and all participants have become, more or less, good practitioners of value theory), the unplanned, nature-like development of economic processes can re-establish itself, at least in secondary form, in the political system. The state must preserve for itself a residue of unconsciousness in order that there accrue to it from its planning functions no responsibilities that it cannot honor without overdrawing its accounts. Thus, economic crisis tendencies continue on the plateau of raising, and expending in a purposive-rational way, the requisite fiscal means.

But, if we do not wish to fall back on theorems of economic crisis, governmental activity can find a *necessary* limit only in available legitimations. As long as motivations remain tied to norms requiring justification, the introduction of legitimate power into the reproduction process means that the "fundamental contradiction" can break out in a questioning, rich in practical consequences, of the norms that still underlie administrative action. And such questioning will break out if the corresponding themes, problems, and arguments are not spared through sufficiently sedimented pre-determinations. Because the economic crisis has been intercepted and transformed into a systematic overloading of the public budget, it has put off the mantle of a natural fate of society. If governmental crisis management fails, it lags behind programmatic demands *that it has placed on itself.* The penalty for this failure is withdrawal of legitimation. Thus, the scope for action contracts precisely at those moments in which it needs to be drastically expanded.

Underlying this crisis theorem is the general reflection that a social identity determined indirectly, through the capability of securing-system integration, is constantly vulnerable on the basis of class structures. For the problematic consequences of the processed and transformed fundamental contradiction of social production for non-generalizable interests are concentrated, as O'Connor tries to show, in the focal region of the stratified raising and particularistic employment of the scarce quantities of taxes that a policy of crisis avoidance exhausts and overdraws. On the one hand, administrative and fiscal filtering of economically conditioned crisis tendencies makes the fronts of repeatedly fragmented class oppositions less comprehensible. The class compromise weakens the organizational capacity of the latently continuing classes. On the other hand, scattered secondary conflicts also become more palpable, because they do not appear as objective systemic crises, but directly provoke questions of legitimation. This explains the functional necessity of making the administrative system, as far as possible, independent of the legitimating system.

This end is served by the separation of instrumental functions of the administration from expressive symbols that release an unspecific readiness to follow. Familiar strategies of this kind are the personalization of substantive issues, the symbolic use of hearings, expert judgments, juridical incantations, and also the advertising techniques (copied from oligopolistic competition) that at once confirm and exploit existing structures of prejudice and that garnish certain contents positively, others negatively, through appeals to feeling, stimulation of unconscious motives,[1] etc. The public realm [*Öffentlichkeit*], set up for effective legitimation, has above all the function of directing attention to topical areas—that is, of pushing *other* themes, problems, and arguments below the threshold of attention and, thereby, of withholding them from opinion-formation. The political system takes over tasks of ideology planning (Luhmann). In so doing, maneuvering room is, to be sure, narrowly limited, for the cultural system is peculiarly resistant to administrative control. *There is no administrative production of meaning.* Commercial production and administrative planning of symbols exhausts the normative force of counterfactual validity claims. The procurement of legitimation is self-defeating as soon as the mode of procurement is seen through.

Cultural traditions have their own, vulnerable, conditions of reproduction. They remain "living" as long as they take shape in an unplanned, nature-like manner, or are shaped with hermeneutic consciousness. (Whereby hermeneutics, as the scholarly interpretation and application of tradition, has the peculiarity of breaking down the nature-like character of tradition as it is handed on and, nevertheless, of retaining it at a reflective level.)[2] The critical appropriation of tradition destroys this nature-like character in discourse. (Whereby the peculiarity of critique consists in its double function[3]: to dissolve analytically, or in a critique of ideology, validity claims that cannot be discursively redeemed; but, at the same time, to release the semantic potentials of the tradition.)[4] To this extent, critique is no less a form of appropriating tradition than hermeneutics. In both cases appropriated cultural contents retain their imperative force, that is, they guarantee the continuity of a history through which individuals and groups can identify with themselves and with one another. A cultural tradition loses precisely this force as soon as it is objectivistically prepared and strategically employed. In both cases conditions for the reproduction of cultural traditions are damaged, and the tradition is undermined. This can be seen in the museum-effect of a hedonistic historicism, as well as in the wear and tear that results from the exploitation of cultural contents for administrative or market purposes. Apparently, traditions can retain legitimizing force only as long as they are not torn out of interpretive systems that guarantee continuity and identity.

The structural dissimilarity between areas of administrative action and areas of cultural tradition constitutes, then, a systematic limit to attempts to compensate for legitimation deficits through conscious manipulation. Of course, a crisis argument can be constructed from this only in connection with the broader point that the expansion of state activity produces the side effect of a disproportionate increase in the need for legitimation. I consider a disproportionate increase probable, not only because the expansion of administratively processed matters makes necessary mass loyalty for new functions of state activity, but because the boundaries of the political system *vis-à-vis* the cultural system shift as a result of this expansion. In this situation, cultural affairs that were taken for granted, and that were previously boundary conditions for the political system, fall into the administrative planning area. Thus, traditions withheld from the public problematic, and all the more from practical discourses, are thematized. An example of such direct administrative processing of cultural tradition is educational planning, especially curriculum planning. Whereas school administrations formerly merely had to codify a canon that had taken shape in an unplanned, nature-like manner, present curriculum *planning* is based on the premise that traditional patterns could as well be otherwise. Administrative planning produces a universal pressure for legitimation in a sphere that was once distinguished precisely for its power of self-legitimation.[5] Other examples of the indirect perturbation of matters taken culturally for granted can be found in regional and city planning (private ownership of land), in planning the health system ("classless hospital"), and, finally, in family planning and marriage laws (which relax sexual taboos and lower the thresholds of emancipation). The end effect is a consciousness of the contingency, not only of the *contents* of tradition, but also of the techniques of tradition, that is, of socialization. Formal schooling is competing with family upbringing as early as at the pre-school age. The problematization of childrearing routines can be seen in the popular pedagogical [*volkspädagogischen*] tasks that schools are assuming through parental rights and individual consultations, as well as in the pedagogical-psychological, scientific journalism on the subject.[6]

At every level, administrative planning produces unintended unsettling and publicizing effects. These effects weaken the justification potential of traditions that have been flushed out of their nature-like course of development. Once their unquestionable character has been destroyed, the stabilization of validity claims can succeed only through discourse. The stirring up of cultural affairs that are taken for granted thus furthers the politicization of areas of life previously assigned to the private sphere. But this development signifies danger for the civil privatism that is secured informally through the structures of the public realm. Efforts at participation and the plethora of alternative models—especially in cultural spheres such as school and university, press, church, theater, publishing, etc.—are indicators of this danger, as is the increasing number of citizens' initiatives.[7]

Demands for, and attempts at, participatory planning can also be explained in this context. Because administrative planning increasingly affects the cultural system—that is, the deep-seated representations of norms and values of those affected—and renders traditional attitudes uncertain, the threshold of acceptability changes. In order to carry through innovations in the planning process, the administration experiments with the participation of those affected. Of course, the functions of participation in governmental planning are ambivalent.[8] Gray areas arise in which it is not clear whether the need for conflict regulation is increased or decreased by participation. The more planners place themselves under the pressure of consensus-formation in the planning process, the more likely is a strain that goes back to two contrary motives: excessive demands resulting from legitimation claims that the administration cannot satisfy under conditions of an asymmetrical class compromise; and conservative resistance to planning, which contracts the horizon of planning and lowers the degree of innovation possible. Socio-psychologically viewed, both motives can be integrated into the same antagonistic interpretive pattern. Thus, analytically separable types of opposition can be represented by the same group. For this reason, laying claim to the "labor power of participation" (Naschold) is an extreme and, for the administration, risky means of meeting legitimation deficits.

These arguments lend support to the assertion that advanced-captialist societies fall into legitimation difficulties. But are they sufficient to establish the insolubility of legitimation problems, that is, do they lead necessarily to the prediction of a legitimation crisis? Even if the state apparatus were to succeed in raising the productivity of labor and in distributing gains in productivity in such a way that an economic growth free of crises (if not disturbances) were guaranteed, growth would still be achieved in accord with priorities that take shape as a function, not of generalizable interests of the population, but of private goals of profit maximization. The patterns of priorities that Galbraith analyzed from the point of view of "private wealth versus public poverty" [9] result from a class structure that is, as usual, kept latent. In the final analysis, *this class structure* is the source of the legitimation deficit.

We have seen now that the state cannot simply take over the cultural system, and that expansion of the areas of state planning actually makes problematic matters that were formerly culturally taken for granted. "Meaning" is a scarce resource and is becoming ever scarcer. Consequently, expectations oriented to use values—that is, expectations monitored by success—are rising in the civil public. The rising level of demand is proportional to the growing need for legitimation. The fiscally siphoned-off resource "value" must take the place of the scanty resource "meaning." Missing legitimation must be offset by rewards conforming to the system. A legitimation crisis arises as soon as the demands for such rewards rise faster than the avialable quantity of value, or when expectations arise that cannot be satisfied with such rewards.

But why should not the levels of demand keep within the boundaries of the operating capacity of the political-economic system? It could, after all, be that the rate of the rise in level of demand is such that it forces on the steering and maintenance systems precisely those processes of adaptation and learning possible within the limits of the existing mode of production. The obvious post-war development of advanced-capitalist societies supports the view that this has already occurred.[10] As long as the welfare-state program, in conjunction with a widespread, techno-cratic common consciousness (which, in case of doubt, makes inalterable system restraints responsible for bottlenecks) can main-tain a sufficient degree of civil privatism, legitimation needs *do not have to* culminate in a crisis.

Offe and his collaborators question whether the form of procur-ing legitimation does not make it necessary for competing parties to outbid one another in their programs and thereby raise the expectations of the population ever higher and higher. This could result in an unavoidable gap between the level of pretension and the level of success, which would lead to disappointments among the voting public.[11] The competitive democratic form of legitima-tion would then generate costs that it could not cover. Assuming that this argument could be sufficiently verified empirically, we would still have to explain why formal democracy has to be retained at all in advanced-capitalist societies. If one considers only the functional conditions of the administrative system, it could as well be replaced by variants: a conservative-authoritarian welfare state that reduces political participation of citizens to a harmless level; or a fascist-authoritarian state that holds the population by the bit at a relatively high level of permanent mobilization without having to overdraw its account through welfare-state measures. Both variants are, in the long run, obviously less compatible with developed captialism than the constitution of a mass democracy with government by parties, for the socio-cultural system produces demands that cannot be met in authoritarian systems.

This reflection supports my thesis that only a rigid socio-cultural system, incapable of being randomly functionalized for the needs of the administrative system, could explain a sharpening of legitima-tion difficulties into a legitimation crisis. A legitimation crisis can be predicted only if expectations that cannot be fulfilled either with the available quantity of value or, generally, with rewards con-forming to the system are systematically produced. A legitimation crisis then, must be based on a motivation crisis—that is, a discrepancy between the need for motives declared by the state, the educational system and the occupational system on the one hand, and the motivation supplied by the socio-cultural system on the other.

Chapter 7.   Theorems of Motivation Crisis

I speak of a motivation crisis when the socio-cultural system changes in such a way that its output becomes dysfunctional for the state and for the system of social labor. The most important motivation contributed by the socio-cultural system in advanced-capitalist societies consists of syndromes of civil and familial-vocational privatism. Civil privatism here denotes an interest in the steering and maintenance [*Versorgung*] performances of the administrative system but little participation in the legitimizing process, albeit participation appropriate to institutionally provided opportunities (high-output orientation versus low-input orientation). Civil privatism thus corresponds to the structures of a depoliticized public realm. Familial-vocational privatism complements civil privatism. It consists in a family orientation with developed interests in consumption and leisure on the one hand, and in a career orientation suitable to status competition on the other. This privatism thus corresponds to the structures of educational and occupational systems that are regulated by competition through achievement.

Both patterns of motivation are important to the continued existence of the political and economic systems. To defend the statement that these patterns of orientation are being systematically destroyed, we must assume the burden of proof for two independent theses. First, we must demonstrate the erosion of traditions in the context of which these attitudes were previously produced. Second, we must show that there are no functional equivalents for the spent traditions, for they are precluded by the logic of development of normative structures. In coordinating motivational patterns with stable traditional cultural patterns, I start with the oversimplified assumption that attitudinal syndromes typical of a society must somehow be represented at the level of socially effective cultural value systems. I also rely on a correspondence of meaning structures at the levels of interpreted needs and cultural tradition.[1] In doing so, I neglect not only subcultural differences, but also the important sociological question, whether—and if so how—cultural patterns are reflected in personality structures through agencies of socialization and practices of childrearing.[2] Above all, I neglect the psychological question: of what components do very complex motivational patterns, introduced only from the point of view of functional imperatives, consist? For the rest, familial-vocational privatism, which crystallizes around the well delimited achievement motive, is positively determined; while civil privatism delimits attitudes only negatively, namely, on the basis of deficient contributions to will-formation.[3]

Privatistic motivational patterns can be coordinated with cultural patterns that represent a peculiar mixture of pre-capitalist and bourgeois elements of tradition. Motivational structures necessary for bourgeois society are only incompletely reflected in bourgeois ideologies. Capitalist societies were always dependent on cultural boundary conditions that they could not themselves reproduce; they fed parasitically on the remains of tradition. This is true above all of the syndrome of civil privatism. On the one hand, as far as expectations *vis-à-vis* the administrative system are concerned, civil privatism is determined by traditions of bourgeois formal law. On the other hand, with regard to a rather passive attitude *vis-à-vis* processes of will-formation, it remains tied to the traditionalistic civic ethic or, even, to familial orientations. Almond and Verba have shown that the conditions of stability in formal democracies can be met only through a "mixed" political culture. The political theories of the bourgeois revolutions demanded active civil partici-pation in a democratically organized will-formation.[4] However, bourgeois democracies, the old as well as the new type, require supplementation by a political culture that screens participatory behavioral expectations out of bourgeois ideologies and replaces them with authoritarian patterns remaining from pre-bourgeois traditions. Almond and Verba speak of a fusion of bourgeois with traditional and familial forms of political culture. Engagement and rationality find therein a counterbalance in particularism and a subordinate mentality.

> If elites are to be powerful and make authoritative decisions, then the involvement, activity, and influence of the ordinary man must be limited. The ordinary citizen must turn power over to elites and let them rule. The need for elite power requires that the ordinary citizen be relatively passive, uninvolved, and deferential to elites. Thus the democratic citizen is called on to pursue contradictory goals; he must be active, yet passive; involved, yet not too involved, influential, yet deferential.[5]

The other motivational syndrome, familial-vocational privatism, can be analyzed from analogous points of view. On the one hand, it is determined by the specifically bourgeois value orientations of possessive individualism and Benthamite utilitarianism.[6] On the other hand, the achievement-oriented vocational ethos of the middle class, as well as the fatalism of the lower class, need to be secured by religious traditions. These traditions are transposed into educational processes through corresponding family structures and techniques of childrearing. The educational processes lead to motivational structures that are class specific, that is, to the repressive authority of conscience and an individualistic achievement orientation among the bourgeoisie, and to external superego structures and a conventional work morality in the lower class. The "Protestant ethic," with its emphasis on self-discipline, secularized vocational ethos, and renunciation of immediate gratification, is no less based on tradition than its traditionalistic counterpart of uncoerced obedience, fatalism, and orientation to immediate gratification. These traditions cannot be renewed on the basis of bourgeois society alone.

Bourgeois culture as a whole was never able to reproduce itself from itself. It was always dependent on motivationally effective supplementation by traditional world-views. Religion, having retreated into the regions of subjective belief, can no longer satisfy neglected communicative needs, even in conjunction with the secular components of bourgeois ideology (that is, an empiricist or rationalist theory of knowledge, the new physics, and the universalistic value systems of modern natural law and utilitarianism). Genuinely bourgeois ideologies, which live only from their own substance,

—offer no support, in the face of the basic risks of existence (guilt, sickness, death) to interpretations that overcome contingency; in the face of individual needs for wholeness [*Heilsbedürfnisse*], they are disconsolate;

—do not make possible human relations with a fundamentally objectivated nature (with either outer nature or one's own body);

—permit no intuitive access to relations of solidarity within groups or between individuals;

—allow no real political ethic; in any case, in political and social life, they accommodate an objectivistic self-interpretation of acting subjects.

Only bourgeois art, which has become autonomous in the face of demands for employment extrinsic to art,[7] has taken up positions on behalf of the victims of bourgeois rationalization. Bourgeois art has become the refuge for a satisfaction, even if only virtual, of those needs that have become, as it were, illegal in the material life-process of bourgeois society. I refer here to the desire for a mimetic relation with nature; the need for living together in solidarity outside the group egoism of the immediate family; the longing for the happiness of a communicative experience exempt from imperatives of purposive rationality and giving scope to imagination as well as spontaneity. Bourgeois art, unlike privatized religion, scientistic philosophy, and strategic-utilitarian morality, did not take on tasks in the economic and political systems. Instead it collected residual needs that could find no satisfaction within the "system of needs." Thus, along with moral universalism, art and aesthetics (from Schiller to Marcuse) are explosive ingredients built into the bourgeois ideology.[8]

I would like to divide into four steps the proof for the assertion that the socio-cultural system will not be able, in the long run, to reproduce the privatistic syndrome necessary for the continued existence of the system. I would like to make plausible (*a*) that the remains of pre-bourgeois traditions, in which civil and familial-vocational privatism are embedded, are being non-renewably dismantled; and (b) that core components of bourgeois ideology, such as possessive individualism and achievement orientation, are being undermined by changes in the social structure. I would then like to show (c) that the, as it were, denuded normative structures, that is, residues of world-views in bourgeois culture—which I find in communicative morality on the one hand and in the tendencies to a post-auratic art on the other—allow no functional equivalents for the destroyed motivational patterns of privatism. Finally, it must be shown (d) that the structures of bourgeois culture, stripped of their traditionalist padding and deprived of their privatistic core, are nonetheless still relevant for motive-formation, and are not simply being pushed to one side as a façade. Motivations important for continued existence can in no way be produced entirely independently of these enfeebled, or only limitedly effective, cultural traditions. Naturally, my goal in this connection too is merely to collect arguments and indicators for future empirical testing. I shall restrict myself to a few very general catchwords.

a) The components of traditional world-views, which represented the context of and the supplement to bourgeois ideologies, were softened and increasingly dissolved in the course of capitalist development. This was due to their incompatibility with generalized social-structural forces of the economic and administrative systems, on the one hand, and with the cognitive attitudes proceeding from the system of science on the other. *Social-structural discrepancies* are a matter of problematic consequences of the expansion of areas of strategic-utilitarian action. Since Max Weber these tendencies have been examined from the point of view of the rationalization of areas of life once regulated by tradition.[9] The advanced-capitalist development of subsystems of purposive-rational action (and the corresponding drying-up of communicative zones of action) is, among other things, the consequence of first, a scientization of professional practice; second, expansion of the service sector through which more and more interactions were subsumed under the commodity form; third, administrative regulation and legalization of areas of political and social intercourse previously regulated informally; fourth, commercialization of culture and politics; and, finally, scientizing and psychologizing processes of childrearing.

On the other hand, there exist *cognitive dissonances* between traditional world-views in the process of dissolution and the imperatives of the scientific system made binding through generalized formal schooling and congealed to a behaviorally effective syndrome in a kind of positivistic common consciousness. Three trends seem to me (with the necessary overgeneralization) to be characteristic today of the structural alterations in world-views. *First,* dominant elements of the cultural tradition are losing the character of world-views, that is, of interpretations of the world, nature, and history as a whole. The cognitive claim to reproduce a totality is surrendered to changing popular syntheses of isolated items of scientific information on the one hand, and, on the other, to an art that retreats esoterically or passes over into life in a desublimated manner. *Further,* attitudes of belief, which since Protestantism have been extensively detached from cult practice, have once again been subjectivistically broken. The liberal disposition of taking-for-true [*Fürwahrhalten*], which is relativized from the start by the taking-for-true of another persuasion, corresponds to the recognition of a pluralism of competing beliefs that is undecided as to truth. Practical questions no longer admit of truth; values are irrational. *Finally,* moral conceptions have been detached from theoretical systems of interpretation. Bourgeois egoism, which became general as a utilitarian secular ethic, has detached itself from foundations in natural law and become unproblematic as "common sense." Since the middle of the nineteenth century, this process has become conscious as the "sublation" [*Aufhebung*] of religion and philosophy, a highly ambivalent process. Religion today is no longer even a personal matter; but in the atheism of the masses, the utopian contents of tradition are also threatened. Philosophy has been stripped of its metaphysical pretension; but in the ruling scientism, those constructions before which a wretched reality must justify itself have also fallen apart.

b) The components of bourgeois ideologies directly relevant to privatistic orientations are also losing their basis through social change.

Achievement Ideology [*Leistungsideologie*]. According to bourgeois conceptions that have remained constant from the beginnings of modern natural law to contemporary election speeches, social rewards should be distributed on the basis of individual achievement. The distribution of gratifications should be an isomorphic image of the achievement differentials of all individuals.[10] The precondition for this is equal opportunity to participate in a competition that is regulated so as to neutralize external influences. The market was such an allocation mechanism. Since it has been recognized, even among the population at large, that social force is exercised in the forms of economic exchange, the market has lost its credibility as a fair (from the perspective of achievement) mechanism for the distribution of life opportunities conforming to the system. Thus, in more recent versions of the achievement ideology, occupational success mediated through formal schooling takes the place of success in the market. This version, however, can claim credibility for itself only if the following conditions are met:

—equal opportunity for admission to higher education;
—non-discriminatory standards of evaluation for performance in school;
—synchronous developments of the educational and occupational systems;
—labor processes whose material structure permits evaluation according to individually accountable achievements.

While educational justice, in terms of opportunities for admission and standards of evaluation, may have increased in all advanced-capitalist countries since World War II,[11] a countertendency can be observed in the other two dimensions. The expansion of the educational system is becoming increasingly independent of changes in the occupational system. Consequently, the connection between formal schooling and occupational success may become looser in the long run.[12] At the same time, there are more and more areas in which production structures and labor processes make evaluation according to individually accountable achievement increasingly improbable; instead, the extrafunctional elements of professional roles are becoming more and more important for conferring occupational status.[13]

Furthermore, fragmented and monotonous labor processes are increasingly penetrating even those sectors in which an identity could previously be formed through the occupational role. Intrinsic motivation to achieve is less and less supported by the structure of labor processes in spheres of labor dependent on the market. An instrumentalist attitude to labor is spreading even in traditional bourgeois vocations (middle- and higher-level employees, professionals). An extrinsic motivation to achieve can, however, be adequately stimulated by wage income only

—if the reserve army exercises an effective competitive pressure on the labor market;

—if there exist sufficient income differentials between the lower-paid groups and the inactive labor population.

Neither condition is automatically fulfilled today. Even in capitalist countries with chronic unemployment (USA), the division of the labor market (into organized sectors and competitive sectors) interferes with the nature-like competitive mechanism. In the subproletarian strata (O'Connor's "surplus labor force") a rising "poverty line" (recognized by the welfare state) has tended to equalize the standards of living of the lower-income groups and groups temporarily released from the labor process. In this way (as well as through resocialization performances for the sick and the criminal), the spurs to competition for status are weakened in the lower strata.

Possessive individualism. Historically, bourgeois society understood itself as an instrumental group that accumulated social wealth only by way of private wealth, that is, which secured economic growth and general welfare through competition between strategically acting private persons. Under these conditions, collective goals could be realized only through possessive-individualistic orientations to gain. This preference system presupposed, naturally,

—that the private economic subjects could, in a subjectively unambiguous way, recognize and calculate needs that remained constant for a given time;

—that these needs could be satisfied with individually demandable goods (as a rule, with monetary rewards conforming to the system).

In developed capitalist societies, neither presupposition is any
longer fulfilled as a matter of course. These societies have attained a
level of social wealth at which it is no longer a question of averting
a few fundamental risks to life and satisfying basic needs. Hence
the individualistic preference system is unclear. In the expanded
horizon of possible satisfying alternatives, prejudgments that can be
monologically ascertained no longer suffice. Socialized upper-class
culture, which once provided self-evident orientations for new
consumption opportunities, no longer sets the standards (notwithstanding national differences). The constant interpretation and
reinterpretation of needs has become a matter of collective
will-formation. In this process, free communication can be replaced
only by massive manipulation, that is, by strong, indirect control.
The more freedom the preference system has, the more pressing
become the problems of market policy for the suppliers. This is
true, at least, if the appearance that consumers can decide privately
and autonomously—that is, according to monologically certain
preferences—is to be preserved. Opportunistic adaptation of
consumers to market strategies of monopolistic competition is the
ironic form of the consumer autonomy that is supposed to be
maintained as the façade of possessive individualism. Moreover,
collective commodities represent a growing proportion of consumable goods as production is increasingly socialized. Conditions of
urban life in complex societies are becoming more and more
dependent on an infrastructure (transportation, leisure, health care,
education, etc.) that increasingly discards the forms of differential
demand and private appropriation.

Orientation to Exchange Value. Finally, we shall draw attention
here to tendencies that are weakening the socialization effects of
the market, especially, on the one hand, the growth of those
segments of the population who do not reproduce their lives
through income for labor schoolchildren and students, welfare
recipients, those living on annuities, the sick, the criminal, the

armed forces, etc.) and, on the other hand, the spread of areas of activity in which abstract labor is replaced by concrete labor.[14] In addition, with reduced working hours (and increased real income), the relevance leisure pursuits acquire as compared with occupational concerns does not directly privilege those needs that can be satisfied monetarily.

c) The erosion of pre-bourgeois, as of bourgeois, residues of tradition permits normative structures to appear that are unsuited to reproduce civil and familial-vocational privatism. The components of cultural tradition dominant today are crystalized around scientism, post-auratic art, and universalistic morality. In each of these areas, irreversible developments, which have followed an internal logic, have taken place. As a result, cultural barriers have arisen that could be broken through only at the psychological cost of regressions, that is, only with extraordinary motivational burdens. German Fascism is an example of a strenuous attempt at a collectively organized regression of consciousness below the thresholds of fundamental scientistic convictions, modern art, and universalistic legal and moral conceptions.

Scientism. The political consequences of the authority enjoyed by the scientific system in developed societies is ambivalent. On the one hand, traditional attitudes of belief cannot withstand the demand for discursive justification established by modern science. On the other hand, short-lived popular syntheses of isolated pieces of information, which have taken the place of global interpretations, secure the authority of science *in abstracto*. The authority of "science" can thus encompass both the broadly effective critique of arbitrary structures of prejudice and the new esoterics of specialized knowledge and judgment. A scientistic self-affirmation of the sciences can promote a positivistic common consciousness that sustains the public realm. But scientism also sets standards[15] by which it can itself be criticized and convicted of residual dogmatism.[16] Theories of technocracy and of elites, which assert the necessity of institutionalized civil privatism, are not immune to objections, because they too must claim to be theories.

Post-Auratic Art. The consequences of modern art are less ambivalent. The modern trend has radicalized the autonomy of bourgeois art *vis-á-vis* contexts of employment external to art. This development produces, for the first time, a counterculture, arising from the center of bourgeois society itself and hostile to the possessive-individualistic, achievement- and advantage-oriented lifestyle of the bourgeoisie. Bohemianism—first established in Paris, the capital of the nineteenth century[17]—embodied a critical pretension that had appeared unpolemically in the aura of bourgeois art. The "alter ego" of the commodity owner—the "human being," which the bourgeois could at one time encounter in the solitary contemplation of a work of art—thereupon split off from him and confronted him in the artistic avant garde, as a hostile power, at best a seducer. In the artistically beautiful, the bourgeoisie once could experience primarily its own ideals and the redemption, however fictive, of a promise of happiness that was merely suspended in everyday life. But in radicalized art, it soon had to recognize the negation rather than the complement of its social practice. In the aura of the bourgeois work of art—that is, in the cultist enjoyment of the already secularized, museum-ripe shrine—was mirrored a belief in the reality of the beautiful illusion. This belief crumbled along with the aura. The artistic independence of the formalist work of art *vis-à-vis* the art-enjoying public is the form of the new disbelief; and the gap between the avant garde and the bourgeoisie is its confirmation. Under the sign *"l'art pour l'art,"* the autonomism of art is carried to the extreme. The truth thereby comes to light that in bourgeois society art expresses not the promise but the irretrievable sacrifice of bourgeois rationalization, the plainly incompatible experiences and not the esoteric fulfillment of withheld, but merely deferred, gratifications.

Modern art is the shell in which the transformation of bourgeois art into the counterculture was prepared. Surrealism marks the historical moment in which modern art destroyed the shell of the no-longer-beautiful illusion in order to pass desublimated over into life. The leveling of the stages of reality between art and life was not, as Benjamin supposed, first brought about by techniques of mass production and mass reception, although it was accelerated by them. Modern art had already shed the aura of classical bourgeois art by making the process of production evident and presenting itself as something that was produced. But art infiltrates the ensemble of use values only when it surrenders its autonomous status. It can just as easily signify the degeneration of art into propagandistic mass art or into commercialized mass culture as, on the other hand, transform itself into a subversive counterculture. No less ambivalent is adherence to formalist art that, on the one hand, resists pressures for assimilation to market-determined needs and attitudes of consumers—and thus resists a false sublation [*Aufhebung*] of art—but that, on the other hand, remains inaccessible to the masses and thus also prevents exoteric preservation of emphatic experiences—in Benjamin's words, secular illuminations. Whether or not Adorno's prediction proves correct *vis-à-vis* that of Benjamin, as long as avant garde art is not completely deprived of its semantic content and does not share the fate of the more and more powerless religious tradition, it strengthens the divergence between the values offered by the socio-cultural system and those demanded by the political and economic systems.[18]

Universalistic Morality. In the moral system, the safety-catch effect that bourgeois ideologies, divested of those components functional for the system, create for the political and economic systems are naturally clearer than those created by the authority of science and the self-dissolution of modern art. During the early development of civilization, the moral order and the legal order were differentiated. In traditional societies, a civic ethic mediatized the particular tribal and familial loyalties. The duties of the citizen competed with family ties. As the domain of validity of normative systems became broader and more abstract with the emergence of a civic ethic, the power of sanction was in part formalized (legalization), in part internalized (internalization). Of course, the moral system and the legal order were still integrated into a unified interpretive framework of world-views that legitimized authority. As soon, however, as traditional societies entered into a process of modernization, growing complexity resulted in control problems that required that the alteration of social norms be speeded up beyond the tempo intrinsic to the nature-like cultural tradition. Thus arose *bourgeois formal law*, which made it possible to release norm-contents from the dogmatism of mere tradition and to determine them intentionally. Positivized legal norms were, on the one hand, uncoupled from the body of privatized moral norms; on the other hand, they needed to be produced (and justified) according to principles. Whereas abstract law is valid only for the area pacified by the power of the state, the morality of bourgeois private persons, which is also raised to the level of general principles, is not limited by the state of nature that persists among states. Since *morality based on principles* [*prinzipielle Moral*] is sanctioned only through the inner authority of conscience, its conflict with the public morality, still tied to the concrete citizen, is embedded in its claim to universality; the conflict is between the cosmopolitanism of the "human being" and the loyalties of the citizen (which cannot be universalistic as long as international relations are subject to the concrete morality of the more powerful).

If one follows (in the dimensions of universalization and internalization) the developmental logic of global systems of social norms (thus leaving the domain of historical example), resolution of this conflict is *conceivable* only if the dichotomy between in-group and out-group morality disappears, the opposition between morally and legally regulated areas is relativized, and the validity of *all* norms is tied to discursive will-formation. This does not exclude the necessity for compelling norms, since no one can know (today) the degree to which aggressiveness can be curtailed and the voluntary recognition of discursive principles attained. Only at that stage, at present a mere construct, would morality become strictly universal. It would also cease to be "merely" moral in terms of the distinction made between law and morality. Internalization too would only be complete when the principle of the justification of possible principles (that is, the readiness to engage in discursive clarification of practical questions) was alone internalized, but in other respects the continuous interpretation of needs was given over to communication processes.

Liberal capitalism gave, for the first time, binding force to strictly universalistic value systems, for economic exchange had to be universalistically regulated and the exchange of equivalents provided an effective basic ideology to free the state from the traditionalistic mode of justification. In organized capitalism, the foundation of this bourgeois mode of legitimation crumbled, while at the same time new and increased demands for legitimation arose. However, the moral system can no more simply erase the memory of a collectively attained state of moral consciousness, once practical discourses have been permitted, than the scientific system can retreat behind an attained state of cumulative knowledge or block theoretical progress once theoretical discourses have been institutionalized. If the moral and scientific systems follow inner logics, as I am supposing they do, the evolution of morality, like the evolution of science, is dependent on truth.

I would like to illustrate this strong assertion with respect to the non-contingent *transition* (that is, one for which reasons can be provided) *from bourgeois formal law to political universal morality*. In order to satisfactorily differentiate between these two stages of morality based on principles, I shall refer to the corresponding philosophical systematizations.

I draw the distinction between norm and principle (that is, metanorm, from which norms can be generated) by applying the operation of generalization to itself. Furthermore, universal validity is the only formal point of view from which a principle can stand out from other principles. A morality based on principles is thus a system that allows only general norms (that is, norms without exceptions, without privileges, and without limitations on the domain of validity). *Modern natural law* attempted to develop systems of legal norms meeting these criteria. The generality of the norms guaranteeing equality can be insured through the formal nature of legal norms. Formality means that no concrete obligations (such as those in traditional natural law or in ethics), but only abstract permissions are subject to juridical norms. (Actions may not be commanded, but only left to choice or forbidden.) Therefore, the only norms allowed are those that delimit compatible scopes of action in which the individual can pursue his particular interests privately and autonomously, that is, by the unlimited employment of non-penalized means. These interests are themselves morally neutral. Only the legal system as a whole is morally justified with reference to consequences that maximize welfare or freedom for all citizens. To this extent, ethics remains the foundation of legitimation. This is possible because, by delimiting a domain of legal action, formal law by definition also delimits a complementary domain of moral action.

Universalistic utilitarianism represents a moral system that also regulates this domain, in accordance with the same criteria as natural law. According to universalistic utilitarianism, all strategic actions that maximize the pleasure or advantage of an individual are permitted to the extent that they are compatible with the chances of every other individual to maximize his pleasure or his advantage. Utilitarianism clearly falls below the stage of internalization attained in the conventional ethics of duty. Motives for action remain external to the morally responsible subject. If these motives too are to be included in the domain of moral evaluation, it must be established that the only actions that deserve to be called morally good are those that not only agree with general laws, but are motivated *only* by respect for the law (and not empirically by consideration of the consequences of action). *Formalistic ethics* (Kant) binds the criterion of generality of norms to the further criterion of autonomy, that is, independence from contingent motives.

The limits of formalistic ethics can be seen in the fact that inclinations incompatible with duties must be excluded from the domain of the morally relevant, and they must be suppressed. The interpretations of needs that are current at any given contingent stage of socialization must thereby be accepted as given. They cannot be made in turn the object of a discursive will-formation. Only *communicative ethics* guarantees the generality of admissible norms and the autonomy of acting subjects solely through the discursive redeemability of the validity claims with which norms appear. That is, generality is guaranteed in that the only norms that may claim generality are those on which everyone affected agrees (or would agree) without constraint if they enter into (or were to enter into) a process of discursive will-formation. The question of which sectors should, if necessary, be regulated through compromise or formal norms of action can also be made the subject of discussion. Only communicative ethics is universal (and not, as is formalistic ethics, restricted to a domain of private morality separate from legal norms); only communicative ethics guarantees autonomy (in that it carries on the process of the insertion of drive potentials into a communicative structure of action—that is, the socialization process—"with will and consciousness.")

d) If today there exists no functionally adequate agreement between the normative structures that still have imperative force and the political-economic system, motivation crises could still be avoided by uncoupling the cultural system. By "uncoupling" I mean a situation in which culture remains an object of private enjoyment or of professional interest, and is even administratively placed under conservation as a kind of free preserve, but is separated from socialization processes. Apart from the fact that substitutes for tradition to fill in for the "uncoupled" cultural components are not discernible, it can be argued that *fundamental convictions of communicative ethics*, and *experimental complexes of countercultures* in which post-auratic art is incorporated, are today already determining typical socialization processes among several strata, that is, they have achieved motive-forming power. Döbert and Nunner have developed the argument that the "semantic surplus" of the dominant components of cultural tradition is all the more "sued for," that is, relevant for behavior, the less we succeed in finding an unobstrusive solution to the problem of the adolescent phase within the framework of conventionalistic norms. K. Kenniston illustrates the meaning of an unconventional outcome of the adolescent crisis by pointing to the reflective attitude toward socially tendered patterns of interpretation which the youth acquires and which allows him, in coming to terms with these cultural interpretations, to work out his definition of identity for himself.

> We will need to distinguish more sharply than we have done so far between attitudes and belief systems on the one hand and the cognitive frameworks or developmental levels within which any given attitude or belief is held. William James long ago contrasted the once-born and the twice-born; the once-born are those who unreflectively and "innocently" accept the convictions of their childhoods; the twice-born are those who may adhere to exactly the same convictions, but who do so in a different way after a protracted period of doubt, criticism, and examination of those beliefs. Viewed as attitudes, the beliefs of the once-born and the twice-born may be identical, but the mind-set, cognitive framework, or developmental level of the once- and twice-born are extremely different. In other words, we need to examine not only the beliefs men hold, but the *way* they hold them—the complexity, richness, and structure of

their views of the world. Politically and socially, it may be more important that members of a given subculture possess a relativistic view of truth than that they are conservatives or liberals.[19]

With the help of this distinction, I can express my thesis as follows: the components of the cultural tradition that are today dominant (and dysfunctional in their working) are more likely to be reflected at the level of the personality system, the more frequently the form of development of the adolescent crisis forces a "second birth" and prevents a conventional outcome of adolescence. For logical reasons, universalistic value systems and countercultural experiential complexes most readily withstand the explicit testing of tradition. *That* the probability of a conventional form of development of the adolescent crisis is decreasing, can be supported by the following indicators:[20]

—expansion of the educational system is lengthening training periods and making possible for increasing proportions of the population a psycho-social moratorium in early adolescence (from the thirteenth to the sixteenth year) and an extension of this phase (in extreme cases, to the age of 30);
—improved formal schooling of cognitive capacities increases the probability that dissonances between profferred patterns of interpretation and perceived social reality will arise and intensify the problem of identity;
—development of egalitarian family structures and spread of childrearing techniques typical of the middle classes promote processes of socialization that tend to burden youth with adolescent problems;
—loosening of sexual prohibitions made possible by pharmaceutics works itself out (as does the temporary liberation—differentiated according to strata—from directly economic pressures) in such a way that socialization processes free of anxiety, with an expanded scope of experimentation, become more probable for adolescents.

Furthermore, it can be inferred from the presently attained degree of complexity of the role system that in advanced-capitalist societies more and more members have at their disposal basic universalistic qualifications for action within roles. Since a morality based on principle can be credibly offered by tradition only in the form of communicative ethics, which cannot function without conflict in the political-economic system, two outcomes are to be expected from a non-conventional form of development of the adolescent crisis: (1) withdrawal as a reaction to an overloading of personality resources (a behavioral syndrome that Keniston has observed and examined in the "alienated") and (2) protest as a result of an autonomous ego organization that cannot be stabilized under the given conditions (a behavioral syndrome that Keniston has described in his "young radicals").[21]

> That it makes sense to look among the youth for a potential for critique of the system is also confirmed by an inventory, taken at a pre-theoretical level, of syndromes of behavior critical of legitimation and/or apathetic. On the *activist* side are to be found the student movement, revolts by school children and apprentices, pacifists, women's lib. The *retreatist* side is represented by hippies, Jesus-people, the drug subculture, phenomena of undermotivation in school, etc. This broad spectrum of behavioral potentials cannot be explained by recourse to the trivial psychological assumptions made in economic theories of crisis (deprivation leads to protest).[22]

Chapter 8.   *A Backward Glance*

Even if it had been less hastily worked out, the proposed argumentation sketch would not be adequate to answer the questions that must be taken up by a theory of advanced capitalism (see the closing pages of Chapter 1, Part II). I would like, in any event, to claim that it has engendered a certain plausibility for the following global statements.

a) Because the economic system has forfeited its functional autonomy *vis-à-vis* the state, crisis manifestations in advanced capitalism have also lost their nature-like character. In the sense in which I introduced the term, a system crisis is not to be expected in advanced capitalism. Of course, crisis tendencies that appear in its place can be traced back to structures that have resulted from the suppression—successful at first—of the system crisis. By means of this development we can explain the moderation of cyclical economic crises to a permanent crisis that appears, on the one hand, as a matter *already* processed administratively and, on the other hand, as a movement *not yet* adequately controlled administratively. This does not exclude constellations in which crisis management fails, with far-reaching consequences. But the appearance of such constellations can no longer be systematically predicted.

b) Economic crises are shifted into the political system through the reactive-avoidance activity of the government in such a way that supplies of legitimation can compensate for deficits in rationality and extensions of organizational rationality can compensate for those legitimation deficits that do appear. There arises a bundle of crisis tendencies that, from a genetic point of view, represent a hierarchy of crisis phenomena shifted upwards from below. But from the point of view of governmental crisis management, these crisis phenomena are distinguished by being mutually substitutable within certain limits. These limits are determined by, on the one hand, the fiscally available quantity of value—the shortage of which cannot be validly predicted within crisis theory (see *a*)—and on the other by supplies of motivation from the socio-cultural system. The substitutive relation between the scarce resources, value and meaning, is therefore decisive for the prediction of crisis.

c) The less the cultural system is capable of producing adequate motivations for politics, the educational system, and the occupational system, the more must scarce meaning be replaced by consumable values. To the same extent, the patterns of distribution that arise from socialized production for non-generalizable interests are endangered. The definitive limits to procuring legitimation are inflexible normative structures that no longer provide the economic-political system with ideological resources, but instead confront it with exorbitant demands. If this rough diagnosis is correct, a legitimation crisis can be avoided in the long run only if the latent class structures of advanced-capitalist societies are transformed or if the pressure for legitimation to which the administrative system is subject can be removed. The latter, in turn, could be achieved by transposing the integration of inner nature *in toto* to another mode of socialization, that is, by uncoupling it from norms that need justification. I shall discuss this possibility in the final part.

PART III.   On the Logic of Legitimation
Problems

The theorems on the motivation crisis I have discussed are based on two presuppositions. First, with Freud, Durkheim, and Mead, I start from the position that motivations are shaped through the internalization of symbolically represented structures of expectation. The sociological concept of internalization (Parsons) raises a series of problems at the psychological level. Psychoanalytic concepts for learning mechanisms (object choice, identification, internalization of models) have been partly rendered more precisely by numerous empirical investigations of motive-learning in children, partly supplemented by cognitivist views or replaced by learning theory. I cannot take up this matter here. I shall concentrate instead on the second, and stronger, presupposition: that the values and norms in accordance with which motives are formed have an immanent relation to truth [*Wahrheitsbezug*]. Viewed ontogenetically, this means that motivational development, in Piaget's sense, is tied to a cognitively relevant development of moral consciousness, the stages of which can be reconstructed logically, that is, by concepts of a systematically ordered sequence of norm systems and behavioral controls. To the highest stage of moral consciousness there corresponds a universal morality, which can be traced back to fundamental norms of rational speech. *Vis-à-vis* competing ethics, universal morality makes a claim not only to *empirical* superiority (based on the ontogenetically observable hierarchy of stages of consciousness), but to *systematic* superiority as well (with reference to the discursive redemption of its claim to validity). In the present context, only this *systematic aspect* of the claimed truth relation of factually valid norms and values is of interest.

Max Weber's concept of legitimate authority[1] directs our attention to the connection between belief in the legitimacy of orders [*Ordnungen*] and their potential for justification, on the one hand, and to their factual validity on the other. The basis of legitimacy reveals "the ultimate grounds of the 'validity' of a domination, in other words . . . those grounds upon which there are based the claims of obedience made by the master against the 'officials' and of both against the ruled." [2] Because the reproduction of class societies is based on the privileged appropriation of socially produced wealth, all such societies must resolve the problem of distributing the surplus social product inequitably and yet legitimately.[3] They do so by means of structural force, that is, by fixing in a system of observed norms the asymmetrical distribution of legitimate chances to satisfy needs. The factual recognition of such norms does not, of course, rest solely on belief in their legitimacy by those affected. It is also based on fear of, and submission to, indirectly threatened sanctions, as well as on simple compliance engendered by the individual's perception of his own powerlessness and the lack of alternatives open to him (that is, by his own fettered imagination). As soon, however, as belief in the legitimacy of an existing order vanishes, the latent force embedded in the system of institutions is released—either as manifest force from above (which is only a temporary possibility) or in the form of expansion of the scope for participation (in which case the key to the distribution of chances to legitimately satisfy needs, that is, the degree of repression, also changes).

> Naturally, the legitimacy of a system of domination may be treated sociologically only as the probability that to a relevant degree the appropriate attitudes will exist, and the corresponding practical conduct ensue. It is by no means true that every case of submissiveness to persons in positions of power is primarily (or even at all) oriented to this belief. Loyalty may be hypocritically simulated by individuals or by whole groups on purely opportunistic grounds, or carried out in practice for reasons of material self-interest. Or people may submit from individual weakness and helplessness because there is no acceptable alternative. But these considerations are not decisive for the classification of types of domination. What is important is the fact that in a given case the particular claim to legitimacy is to a significant degree, and according to its type, treated as "valid"; that this fact confirms the position of the persons claiming authority and that it helps to determine the choice of means of its exercise.[4]

In contemporary sociology, the usefulness of the concept of legitimation, which permits a demarcation of types of legitimate authority (in Weber's sense) according to the forms and contents of legitimation, is undisputed. What is controversial is the *relation of legitimation to truth*. This relation to truth must be presumed to exist if one regards as possible a motivation crisis resulting from a systematic scarcity of the resource of "meaning." Non-contingent grounds for a disappearance of legitimacy can, that is, be derived only from an "independent" [*eigensinnigen*]—that is, truth-dependent—evolution of interpretive systems that systematically restricts the adaptive capacity of society.

Chapter 1.   Max Weber's Concept of Legitimation

The controversy over the truth-dependency of legitimations was ignited at the sociological level by Max Weber's ambiguous conception of "rational authority," that is, the legally formed and procedurally regulated type of authority characteristic of modern societies.

> Experience shows that in no instance does domination voluntarily limit itself to the appeal to material or affectual or ideal motives as a basis for its continuance. In addition every such system attempts to establish and to cultivate the belief in its legitimacy.[5]

Weber even affirms "the generally observable need of any power, or even of any advantage of life, to justify itself." [6] If belief in legitimacy is conceived as an empirical phenomenon without an immanent relation to truth, the grounds upon which it is explicitly based have only psychological significance. Whether such grounds can sufficiently stabilize a given belief in legitimacy depends on the institutionalized prejudices and observable behavioral dispositions of the group in question. If, on the other hand, every effective belief in legitimacy is assumed to have an immanent relation to truth, the grounds on which it is explicitly based contain a rational validity claim that can be tested and criticized independently of the psychological effect of these grounds. In the first case, only the motivational function of the justificatory grounds can be the object of investigation. In the second, their motivational function cannot be considered independently of their logical status, that is, of their criticizable claim to *motivate rationally*. This is true even if this claim is, as it usually is, counterfactually raised and stabilized.

For the interpretation of rational authority,[7] this alternative means that in the first case an authority will be viewed as legitimate if at least two conditions are fulfilled: (*a*) the normative order must be established positively; and (*b*) those legally associated must believe in its legality, that is, in the formally correct procedure for the creation and application of laws. The belief in legitimacy thus shrinks to a belief in legality; the appeal to the legal manner in which a decision comes about suffices. In the case of the truth-dependency of belief in legitimacy, however, the appeal to the state's monopoly on the creation and application of laws obviously does not suffice. The procedure itself is under pressure for legitimation. At least *one* further condition must therefore be fulfilled: grounds for the legitimizing force of this formal procedure must be given (for example, that the procedural competency lies with a constitutionally constituted state authority).[8]

The first of the aforementioned positions is represented today by Niklas Luhmann:

> The law of a society is positivized when the legitimacy of pure legality is recognized, that is, when law is respected because it is made by responsible decision in accordance with definite rules. Thus, in a central question of human co-existence, arbitrariness becomes an institution.[9]

Luhmann is here following the decisionistic legal theory founded by Carl Schmitt:

> The positivization of law means that legitimate legal validity [*Rechtsgeltung*] can be obtained for any given contents, and that this is accomplished through a decision which confers validity upon the law and which can take the validity from it. Positive law is valid by virtue of decisions.[10]

The formal rules of procedure suffice as legitimizing premises of decision and require for their part no further legitimation, for they fulfill their function—to absorb uncertainty—in any case. They connect the uncertainty as to *which* decision will come about with the certainty that *some* decision will come about.[11] The abstract imperative validity [*Sollgeltung*] of norms that can do without a material justification beyond the following of correct procedure in their origin and application serves "to stabilize behavioral expectations against disappointment and thereby to guarantee structures." [12] Normative validity can, of course, fulfill this function only as long as it remains latent and does not enter explicitly into the sense of the "ought" [*Sollens*]: "Social processes for dealing with disappointment and for learning are presupposed in all norming of behavioral expectations. They cannot, however, be reflected in the normed meaning." [13] It is meaningless to probe behind the factual belief in legitimacy and the validity claim of norms for criticizable grounds of validity. The fiction that one could do so if necessary belongs to the constituents of reliable counterfactual expectations. These, in turn, can be comprehended only from a functionalist point of view, that is, by treating validity claims as functionally necessary deceptions [*Täuschungen*]. The deception may not, however, be exposed if the belief in legality is not to be shaken.[14]

The *second* of the two positions mentioned above is represented by Johannes Winckelmann. He considers formal rationality in Weber's sense an insufficient foundation for legitimation: the belief in legality does not *per se* legitimize. Legal positivism requires, rather, a general consensus grounded in a rational orientation to value [*wertrational begründeten*].[15] "The rational value-oriented postulates form the regulative principles for normative positing [*Setzung*] and its concretization. Only that positing is normatively legitimized . . . which keeps within the bounds of the formal legal principles which are set in this way." [16] Legality can create legitimation when, and only when, grounds can be provided to show that certain formal procedures fulfill material claims to justice under certain institutional boundary conditions. "In principle, the concept of legal authority in Max Weber refers to the rational, and in fact rational *value-oriented, statutory* authority. Only in its degenerate form was this distorted into undignified, value-neutral, purely purposive-rational, formal legal authority." [17] Winckelmann's thesis is questionable from a hermeneutic point of view, because it leads systematically to the conclusion that the rational value-oriented foundations of the belief in legitimacy can be justified [*begründungsfähig*] and criticized. This is incompatible with Max Weber's view of the rationally irresoluble pluralism of competing value systems and beliefs [*Glaubensmächte*].[18] This point is not important in the present context. But from a systematic point of view as well, the assumption of basic *material* norms capable of being justified leads to the difficulty that certain normative contents must be theoretically singled-out. Hitherto, philosophical efforts to rehabilitate traditional or—as Winckelmann himself seems inclined—modern natural law, in whatever version, have proved as unavailing as attempts to found a material value ethics (in the sense of Scheler or Nicolai Hartmann). Moreover, there is no need to accept such a burden of proof in order to demonstrate the criticizability of claims to appropriateness. Recourse to the fundamental norms of rational speech, which we presuppose in every discourse (including practical discourses), is sufficient.

In my debate with Luhmann, I derived the belief in legality from a belief in legitimacy that can be justified.

> The unobjectionable manner in which a norm comes into being, that is, the legal form of a procedure, guarantees as such only that the authorities which the political system provides for, and which are furnished with certain competencies and recognized as competent within that system, bear the responsibility for valid law. But these authorities are part of a system of authority which must be legitimized as a whole if pure legality is to be able to count *as an indication* of legitimacy. In a fascist regime, for example, the legal form of administrative acts can have at best a masking function. This means that the technical legal form alone, pure legality, will not be able to guarantee recognition in the long run if the system of authority cannot be legitimized independently of the legal form of exercising authority. Luhmann admits "that special grounds are required in order for selection performances which rest only on decisions to be accepted." But he believes that through an institutionalized legal form of proceeding, that is, through procedures, "such additional grounds for the recognition of decisions are created

and, in this sense, the power of decision is produced and legitimized, that is, made independent of concretely exercised force." A procedure can, however, legitimize only indirectly, through reference to authorities which, for their part, must be recognized. Thus, the written bourgeois constitutions contain a catalogue of basic rights, strongly immunized against alteration, which has legitimizing force in so far as, and only in so far as, it is understood in conjunction with an ideology of the system of authority. Moreover, the organs which are responsible for making and applying the laws are in no way legitimated by the legality of their modes of procedure, but likewise by a general interpretation which supports the system of authority as a whole. The bourgeois theories of parliamentarianism and of the sovereignty of the people were part of such an ideology. The fundamental misconception of decisionistic legal theory—which is itself subject to the suspicion of ideology—is that the validity of legal norms could be grounded on decisions and only on decisions. But the naive validity claims of norms of action refer in each case (at least implicitly) to the possibility of discursive foundation. If binding decisions are legitimate, that is, if they can be made independently of the concrete exercise of force and of the manifest threat of sanctions, and can be regularly implemented even against the interests of those affected, then they must be considered as the fulfillment of recognized norms. This unconstrained normative validity is based on the supposition that the norm could, if necessary, be justified and defended against critique. And this supposition is itself not automatic. It is the consequence of an interpretation which admits of consensus and which has a justificatory function, in other words, of a world-view which legitimizes authority.[19]

The discussion of the relation to truth of belief in legitimacy was sparked by Max Weber's conception of belief in legality. It has lead meanwhile to problems concerning the possibility of justifying norms of action and evaluation in general; this problem cannot be resolved by sociological means. If the capacity of practical questions for truth could be disputed, the position I defended would be untenable. I shall, therefore, first establish (Chapters 2 and 3) the *possibility* of justifying [*begründen*] normative-validity claims, that is, of providing rational grounds [*rational motivieren*] for their recognition. I shall then go on (Chapter 4) to discuss how matters *actually* stand (in our type of society) with respect to the claim to legitimacy of existing systems of norms: whether the acceptance of binding decisions without grounds has today become routine, or whether functionally requisite motivations are still produced through internalization of norms that need justification.

Chapter 2. The Relation of Practical Questions to Truth

Since Hume the dualism between "is" and "ought," between facts and values, has been thoroughly clarified. It signifies the impossibility of logically deriving prescriptive sentences or value judgments from descriptive sentences or statements.[1] In analytic philosophy this has been the point of departure for a non-cognitivist treatment of practical questions in which we distinguish between empiricist and decisionist lines of argument. They converge in the conviction that moral controversies cannot, in the final analysis, be decided with reason because the value premises from which we infer moral sentences are irrational. The empiricist assumptions are that we employ practical sentences either to express the attitudes and needs of the speaker or to bring about or to manipulate behavioral dispositions in the hearer. In analytic philosophy, primarily semantic and pragmatic investigations of the emotive meaning of moral expressions have been carried out along this line (Stevenson, Monro).[2] The decisionistic assumptions are that practical sentences belong to an autonomous domain that is subject to a logic different from that governing theoretical-empirical sentences and that connected with belief acts or decisions, rather than experiences. In analytic philosophy, primarily logical investigations—into questions of a deontic logic (von Wright) or, generally, into the formal structure of prescriptive languages (Hare)—have arisen from this line of thought.[3]

I shall choose as an example an instructive essay of K. H. Ilting, which connects arguments of both types in order to reject the cognitivist claim to justification of practical sentences. By means of language analysis, Ilting attempts to rehabilitate Carl Schmitt's version of the Hobbesian position.[4] He makes the prior decision— not further grounded—to derive norms from demand sentences

[*Forderungssätzen*] or imperatives. The elementary demand sentence signifies: (*a*) that the speaker wants something to be the case, and (*b*) that he wants the hearer to adopt and to actualize the state of affairs desired by him (p. 97). (*a*) is a definite volition; (*b*) is a demand [*Aufforderung*]. Ilting draws a further distinction between the thought that the demand contains, the appeal to the will of the hearer to adopt this thought and to act according to it, and, finally, the volitional act of the hearer by which he accepts or refuses the appeal. The decision to follow the imperative of another is neither logically nor causally "effected" by the demand; "Only that can be expected to which the hearer is himself inclined or to which he can be moved by the threat of a greater evil" (p. 99). What use the hearer makes of his choice [*Willkür*] in the face of an imperative depends on empirical motives alone.

If two imperatives are connected on the basis of reciprocity in such a way that both parties agree to accede to each other's demands, we speak of a *contract* [*Vertrag*]. A contract is grounded in a norm that both parties to the contract "recognize."

> The recognition of the common norm creates certain behavioral expectations which can make it appear advisable to one of the participants to accomplish something which is in the other's interest. With that, however, the demand that the other for his part now accomplish what has been agreed to ceases to be a mere expectation which he may accept or refuse according to choice (as in the case of an imperative). It becomes a *claim* which he has already previously recognized as a condition of his action (p. 100ff.).

The imperativist construction proposed by Ilting for the reconstruction of systems of norms is favorable to the aims of non-cognitivism. Since the cognitive component of demand sentences (wishes, commands) is limited to the propositional content ("the desired state of affairs," the "thought" which the demand contains), and since volitional acts (decisions, beliefs, attitudes) are motivated only empirically (that is, bring needs and interests into play), as soon as a norm comes into force through the choice [*Willkür*] of the contracting parties, it too can contain nothing that would admit of cognitive support or disputation, that is, of justification or objection.

It would be meaningless to try to "justify" practical sentences otherwise than by reference to the fact of an empirically motivated contractual agreement.

> It is no longer meaningful to look for a justification of the mutually recognized contractual norm. Both parties had a sufficient motive to recognize the contractual norm . . . Just as little can one . . . meaningfully demand a justification of the norm that contractual agreements are to be kept (p. 101).

The proposed construction (whose explicit content, incidentally, might be difficult to reconcile with its own status) is to be evaluated in the light of its aim: to explain as completely as possible the meaning and the achievement of norms. But it cannot at all adequately explain *one* central element of the meaning of norms, namely the "ought" or normative validity. A norm has a binding character—therein consists its validity claim. But if only empirical motives (such as inclinations, interests, and fear of sanctions) sustain the agreement, it is impossible to see why a party to the contract should continue to feel bound to the norms when his original motives change. Ilting's construction is unsuitable because it does not permit us to give an account of the decisive *difference between obeying concrete commands and following intersubjectively recognized norms*. Thus, Ilting finds it necessary to introduce the auxiliary hypothesis "that the recognition of a 'fundamental norm' is always presupposed in the recognition of any other norm; the recognition of a norm is to be regarded as an act of the will which might in the future also be brought to bear against the will itself" (p. 103). But what motive could there be for recognizing such a paradoxical fundamental norm? The validity of norms cannot be grounded on an obligation to oneself not to change them, for the original constellation of interests can change at any time, and norms that are made independent of their interest-basis lack, according to Ilting's own construction, any sense of normative regulation at all. If, on the other hand, one wishes to avoid the difficulty of normatively fixing fleeting constellations of interest for an undetermined time and to allow for revisions, then it must be possible to distinguish valid motives for revision. If any given change in motives is sufficient cause for changing norms, then we cannot plausibly distinguish the validity claim of a norm from the imperative meaning of a demand. If, on the other hand, there can be only empirical motives, one is as good as the other—each is justified by its mere existence. The only motives that can be distinguished from others are those for which we can adduce reasons.

From this reflection, it follows that we cannot explain the validity claim of norms without recourse to rationally motivated agreement or at least to the conviction that consensus on a recommended norm could be brought about *with reasons*. In that case the model of contracting parties who need know only what an imperative means is inadequate. The appropriate model is rather the communication community [*Kommunikationsgemeinschaft*] of those affected, who as participants in a practical discourse test the validity claims of norms and, to the extent that they accept them with reasons, arrive at the conviction that in the given circumstances the proposed norms are "right." The validity claim of norms is grounded not in the irrational volitional acts of the contracting parties, but in the rationally motivated recognition of norms, which may be questioned at any time. The cognitive component of norms is, thus, not limited to the propositional content of the normed behavioral expectations. The normative-validity claim is itself cognitive in the sense of the supposition (however counterfactual) that it could be discursively redeemed—that is, grounded in consensus of the participants through argumentation.

An ethics developed along imperativist lines lacks the proper dimension of possible justification of practical sentences: moral argumentation. As the examples of Max Weber and Karl Popper show, there are certainly positions which leave room for the possibility of moral argument and retain, nevertheless, a decisionistic treatment of the value problematic. The reason for this lies in a narrow concept of rationality that permits only deductive arguments. Since a valid deductive argument can neither produce new information nor contribute anything to the truth-values of its components, moral argumentation is limited to two tasks: analytically testing the consistency of the value premises (or the preference system taken as a basis); and empirically testing the realizability of goals selected from value perspectives. This kind of "rational critique of values" in no way changes the irrationality of the choice of the preference system itself.

Hans Albert goes a step further in the metaethical application of the principles of *critical rationalism*.[5] If—as in critical rationalism—one gives up the idea of justification [*Begründung*] in science, while retaining the fallibilistically interpreted possibility of critical testing, then the renunciation of claims to justification in ethics need not automatically have decisionistic consequences. Because cognitive claims, like practical claims, are subject to rationally motivated evaluation from selected points of view, Albert affirms the possibility of critically testing practical sentences in a somewhat analogous way to that in which theoretical-empirical sentences are tested. Since he involves the "active search for contradictions" in the discussion of value problems, moral argumentation can assume—beyond the tasks of testing the consistency of values and the realizability of goals—the productive task of critically developing values and norms.

> Of course, no value judgment can, as we know, be directly deduced from statements of fact. But certain value judgments can, in the light of revised convictions about the facts, prove to be incompatible with certain value convictions which we previously held . . . From the fact that we discover new moral ideas which make previous solutions to moral problems appear questionable, there can indeed result another kind of critique. In the light of such ideas, certain problematic features of these solutions, which have previously gone unnoticed or been taken as self-evident, often first become perceptible. There results in this way a new problem situation, as happens in science with the appearance of new ideas.[6]

In this way, Albert introduces into Popperian criticism the idea already developed in the pragmatist tradition (especially by Dewey) of a rational clarification and critical development of inherited value systems.[7] To be sure, even this program remains non-cognitivist at its core, because it retains the alternative between decisions, which cannot be rationally motivated, and proofs or justifications, which are possible only through deductive arguments. Even the "bridge principles" introduced *ad hoc* cannot bridge this gap. The idea developed in critical rationalism of renouncing proof or confirmation in favor of the elimination of untruths cannot vindicate the power of discursively attained, rational consensus against the Weberian pluralism of value systems, gods, and demons. The empiricist and/or decisionist barriers, which immunize the so-called pluralism of values against the efforts of practical reason, cannot be overcome so long as the power of argumentation is sought only in the power of refuting deductive arguments.

In contrast, Peirce and Toulmin have both seen the rationally motivating force of argumentation in the fact that the progress of knowledge takes place through substantial arguments.[8] The latter are based on logical inferences, but they are not exhausted in deductive systems of statements. Substantial arguments serve to redeem or to criticize validity claims, whether the claims to truth implicit in assertions or the claims to correctness connected with norms (of action and evaluation) or implied in recommendations and warnings. They have the force to convince the participants in a discourse of a validity claim, that is, *to provide rational grounds for* the recognition of validity claims. Substantial arguments are explanations and justifications, that is, pragmatic unities, in which not sentences but speech acts (sentences employed in utterances) are connected. The systematic aspect of their connection has to be clarified within the framework of a logic of discourse.[9] In theoretical discourses—which serve to ground assertions—consensus is produced according to rules of argumentation different from those obtaining in practical discourses—which serve to justify recommended norms. However, in both cases the goal is the same: a rationally motivated decision about the recognition (or rejection) of validity claims.

What *rationally motivated recognition* of the validity claim of a norm of action means follows from the discursive procedures of motivation. Discourse can be understood as that form of communication that is removed from contexts of experience and action and whose structure assures us that the bracketed validity claims of assertions, recommendations, or warnings are the exclusive object of discussion; that participants, themes and contributions are not restricted except with reference to the goal of testing the validity claims in questions; that no force except that of the better argument is exercised; and that, as a result, all motives except that of the cooperative search for truth are excluded. If under these conditions a consensus about the recommendation to accept a norm arises argumentatively, that is, on the basis of hypothetically proposed, alternative justifications, then this consensus expresses a "rational will." Since all those affected have, in principle, at least the chance to participate in the practical deliberation, the "rationality" of the discursively formed will consists in the fact that the reciprocal behavioral expectations raised to normative status afford validity to a *common* interest ascertained *without deception*. The interest is common because the constraint-free consensus permits only what *all* can want; it is free of deception because even the interpretations of needs in which *each individual* must be able to recognize what he wants become the object of discursive will-formation. The discursively formed will may be called "rational" because the formal properties of discourse and of the deliberative situation sufficiently guarantee that a consensus can arise only through appropriately interpreted, *generalizable* interests, by which I mean needs *that can be communicatively shared*. The limits of a decisionistic treatment of practical questions are overcome as soon as argumentation is expected to test the generaliz*ability* of interests, instead of being resigned to an impenetrable pluralism of apparently ultimate value orientations (or belief-acts or attitudes). It is not the fact of this pluralism that is here disputed, but the assertion that it is impossible to separate by argumentation generalizable interests from those that are and remain particular. Albert mentions, to be sure, various types of more or less contingent "bridge principles." But he does not mention the only principle in which practical reason expresses itself, namely, the principle of universalization.

Only on this principle do cognitivist and non-cognitivist approaches in ethics part ways. In analytic philosophy, the "good-reasons approach" (which begins with the question of the extent to which "better" reasons can be given for action *X* than for action *Y*) has led to the renewal of a strategic-utilitarian, contractual morality that distinguishes fundamental duties by the possibility of their universal validity (Grice).[10] Another line of argument goes back to Kant in order to disconnect the categorical imperative from the context of transcendental philosophy and to reconstruct it, in terms of language analysis, as the "principle of universality" or the "generalization argument" (Baier, Singer).[11] The methodical philosophy of the Erlangen School also understands its theory of moral argument as a renewal of the critique of practical reason (Lorenzen, Schwemmer).[12] In the present context, we are interested less in the proposed norming of the language of discussion permitted in the deliberation of practical questions than in the introduction of the "moral principle" that obliges each participant in a practical discourse to transfer his subjective desires into generalizable desires. Thus Lorenzen also speaks of the principle of *transsubjectivity*.

The introduction of maxims of universalization (of whatever type) raises the consequent problem of the circular justification of a principle that, supposedly, first makes possible the justification of norms. Paul Lorenzen admits to a residual decisionistic problematic when he calls the recognition of the moral principle an "act of faith . . . if one defines faith in a negative sense as the acceptance of something which is not justified." [13] But he removes the arbitrary character of this act of faith insofar as he claims that methodical exercise of the practice of deliberation trains one to a rational attitude. Reason cannot be demonstrated but can, to a certain degree, be inculcated by socialization. Schwemmer gives this interpretation a different turn, if I understand him correctly, in that he has recourse to the prior understanding [*Vorverständnis*] of the intersubjective practice of speaking and acting exercised in unreflected [*naturwüchsigen*] contexts of action, on the one hand, and to the motive arising therein to settle conflicts *without force*, on the other. But methodical philosophy's claim to ultimate foundations makes it necessary for Schwemmer too to stylize a "first" decision:

> The moral principle is established on the basis of a common practice which I have here attempted step by step to motivate and to make understandable. In this common action, we have so transformed our desires that we recognized the common transformation of desires as the fulfillment of our original desires (motives) which brought us to take up a common practice in the first place. What is required for

the common establishment of the moral principles is participation in common practice, to this extent a "decision" which is not justified through further speech. And this participation first makes possible rational action which takes account of and understands the desires of others.[14]

The difficulties in Schwemmer's construction are analyzed in a work by Looser, Uscher, Maciejewski, and Menne:

A necessary condition for beginning the construction of normed speech is that the individuals who make this beginning already stand in a *common* context of speech and action, and agree therein, through a pre-form [*Vorform*] of "practical deliberation" (*Schwemmer*), to undertake *in common* the construction of a well-founded mode of speech. That this anticipation is achieved under unclarified conditions is shown by the fact that the Erlangen attempt does not conceive itself as a historically identified endeavor which could be understood as the consequence of acquiring and pushing through the principle of resolving practical questions in communication free of force, that is, discursively. Instead, the decision between talk and force is itself still placed in the construction of practical philosophy.[15]

The problematic that arises with the introduction of a moral principle is disposed of as soon as one sees that the expectation of discursive redemption of normative-validity claims is already contained in the structure of intersubjectivity and makes specially introduced maxims of universalization superfluous. In taking up a practical discourse, we unavoidably suppose an ideal speech situation that, on the strength of its formal properties, allows consensus only through *generalizable* interests. A cognitivist linguistic ethics [*Sprachethik*] has no need of principles. It is based only on fundamental norms of rational speech that we must always presuppose if we discourse at all. This, if you will, transcendental character of ordinary language, which is also implicitly claimed by the Erlangen School as the basis for the construction of normed speech, can (as I hope to show) be reconstructed in the framework of a universal pragmatic.[16]

*Chapter 3.   The Model of the Suppression of
              Generalizable Interests*

Our excursion into the contemporary discussion of ethics was
intended to support the assertion that practical questions admit of
truth. If this is so, justifiable norms can be distinguished from norms
that merely stabilize relations of force. Insofar as norms express
generalizable interests, they are based on a *rational consensus* (or
they would find such a consensus if practical discourse could take
place). Insofar as norms do not regulate generalizable interests,
they are based on force [*Gewalt*]; in the latter context we use the
term normative power [*Macht*].

There is, however, one case of normative power that is distinguished by being indirectly justifiable: *compromise*. A normed
adjustment between particular interests is called a compromise if it
takes place under conditions of a balance of power between the
parties involved. The separation of powers is an ordering principle
intended to guarantee such a balance of power in the domain of
particular interests in order to make compromises possible. Another
ordering principle is realized in bourgeois civil law, which delimits
autonomous domains of action for the strategic pursuit of individual
interests. It presupposes a balance of power between private
persons and makes compromises on non-generalizable interests
unnecessary. In both cases, universalistic principles that admit of
justification are employed—with the proviso, to be sure, that the
generalizability of the regulated interests can be denied. This
proviso can, in turn, be tested only through discourse. For this
reason, separation of powers and democracy are not of equal rank
as political-ordering principles.

That democratic will-formation turns into repression if it is not
kept within limits by the freedom-guaranteeing principle of the
separation of powers, is a theme of the counter-enlightenment that
was renewed by Helmut Schelsky in connection with the German
federal elections of November, 1972:

> According to its oft declared, fundamental political constitution, the
> Federal Republic represents a harmony of both principles in a
> liberal-democratic [*freiheitlich-demokratischen*] order. It is perhaps

no accident that the principle of freedom precedes that of democracy in this formula. But if those in power then programmatically announce the priority of "more democracy" in this fundamental order based on principles, then the acceptance of "less freedom" is tacitly, and without admitting it, bound up with that program.[1]

The gravity of this dilemma disappears as soon as we see that: (a) separation of powers may legitimately be introduced only where the domains of interests to be regulated cannot be justified discursively and thus require compromises; and that (b) demarcating particular from generalizable interests in a manner that admits of consensus is possible only by means of discursive will-formation. Counter to the Schelsky's diagnosis furthermore, it is the Social Democrats who—with the postulate of "equal rights for labor and capital"—are reclaiming, for example, separation of powers in a domain of interests that was, to be sure, previously removed from discursive will-formation, but in which there is certainly no lack of generalizable interests. Even if a "class-compromise" came about in advanced capitalism under conditions of a balance of power, the justifiability of the compromise would remain questionable as long as it excluded the possibility of discursively testing whether it was in fact a matter, on both sides, of particular interests that did not permit of a rational will and were thus accessible only to compromise.

A compromise can be justified as a compromise only if both conditions are met: a balance of power among the parties involved and the non-generalizability of the negotiated interests exist. If even one of these *general* conditions of *compromise formation* is not fulfilled, we are dealing with a pseudo-compromise [*Scheinkompromiss*]. In complex societies *pseudo-compromises* are an important form of legitimation. But historically they are not the rule. In traditional and liberal-capitalist societies, it is rather the *ideological form* of justification, which either asserts or counterfactually supposes a generalizability of interests, that is dominant. In this case, legitimations consist of interpretations, of narrative presentations or (for example in natural law) of systematized explanations and chains of argument, that have the double function of proving that the validity claims of norm systems are legitimate and of avoiding thematization and testing of discursive-validity claims. The specific achievement of such ideologies consists in the inconspicuous manner in which communication is systematically limited.[2] A social theory critical of ideology can, therefore, identify the normative power built into the institutional system of a society only if it starts from the *model of the suppression of generalizable interests* and compares normative structures existing at a given time with the hypothetical state of a system of norms formed, *ceteris paribus,* discursively. Such a counterfactually projected reconstruction—for which P. Lorenzen proposes the procedure of "normative genesis"[3]—can be guided by the question (justified, in my opinion, by considerations from universal pragmatics): how would the members of a social system, at a given stage in the development of productive forces, have collectively and bindingly interpreted their needs (and which norms would they have accepted as justified) if they could and would have decided on organization of social intercourse through discursive will-formation, with adequate knowledge of the limiting conditions and functional imperatives of their society?[4] Of course, the model of the suppression of generalizable interests—which explains at one and the same time the *functional necessity* of the apparent legitimation of domination and the *logical possibility* of undermining normative-validity claims by a critique of ideology—can be made fruitful for social theory only by making empirical assumptions.

We can start from the position that the orientation of action toward institutionalized values is unproblematic only as long as the normatively prescribed distribution of opportunities for the legitimate satisfaction of needs rests on an actual consensus. But as soon as a difference of opinion arises, the "injustice" of the repression of generalizable interests can be recognized in the categories of the interpretive system obtaining at the time. This consciousness of conflicts of interest is, as a rule, sufficient motive for replacing value-oriented action with interest-guided action. The pattern of communicative action gives way then, in politically relevant domains of behavior, to that type of behavior for which the competition for scarce goods supplies the model, that is, strategic action. Thus, I use the term "interests" for needs that are—to the extent of the withdrawal of legitimation and the rising of the consciousness of conflict—rendered subjective and detached, as it were, from the crystallizations of commonly shared values supported by tradition (and made binding in norms of action).

These assumptions of conflict theory can be connected with the discourse model at two levels. I make the empirical assumption that the interest constellations of the parties involved, which are revealed in cases of conflict, coincide sufficiently with interests that would have to find expression among those involved if they *were* to enter into practical discourse. Furthermore, I make the methodological assumption that it is meaningful and possible to reconstruct (even for the normal case of norms recognized without conflict) the hidden interest positions of involved individuals or groups by counterfactually imagining [*fingieren*] the limit case of a conflict between the involved parties in which they would be forced to consciously perceive their interests and strategically assert them, instead of satisfying basic interests simply by actualizing institutional values as is normally the case. Marx too had to make these or equivalent assumptions in the analysis of class struggles. He had: (*a*) to draw a general distinction between particular and general interests; (*b*) to understand the consciousness of justified and, at the same time, suppressed interests as a sufficient motive for conflict; and (*c*) to attribute, with reason, interest positions to social groups. The social scientist can only hypothetically project this ascription of interests; indeed a direct confirmation of this hypothesis would be possible only in the form of a practical discourse among the very individuals or groups involved. An indirect confirmation on the basis of observable conflicts is possible to the extent that the ascribed interest positions can be connected with predictions about conflict motivations.

Claus Offe provides an instructive survey of alternative attempts to "establish a critical standard for determining the selectivity of a political system and thereby to avoid the complementary difficulties of systems-theoretic and of behavioristic procedures (which are unable to conceptualize the non-events of suppressed, that is, latent, claims and needs.)" [5] Three of the alternatives mentioned are, for essential and easily seen reasons, inapplicable.

—"A need potential can be defined *anthropologically*. The totality of unfulfilled needs appears then as a non-fact, as an indicator of the selectivity of a political system, of its greater or lesser character of domination" (p. 85). None of the drive theories put forward until now, however, has succeeded even in making it plausible that the assumption of an invariant need structure in human beings is both meaningful and empirically testable. Through the example of the most prominent and well-thought-out drive theory, namely, the psychoanalytic, it can be convincingly shown, in my opinion, that theoretical predictions about the range of variation of aggressive and libidinal drive potentials are not possible.[6]

—In the framework of an *objectivistic philosophy of history*, the attribution of interests can be projected on the basis of observable structural features. However, teleological historical constructions acquiesce in a circular structure of proof and, for this reason, cannot make their empirical reference plausible.

Such a method, which only supposedly stands in the succession of Marxist "orthodoxy," runs the danger of raising to a theoretical premise what is to be demonstrated by analysis (the class character of the organizations of political domination) and, at the same time, of reducing to insignificance the historical particularities of the selectivity of a concrete institutional system—whether or not it can be brought into agreement with the dogmatically advanced class concept (p. 86ff.).

—Finally, there is the *normative-analytic* approach, which is dependent upon declared options for more or less conventionally introduced goal states. Social-scientific systems analysis proceeds normatively in this sense, since there is as yet no theory that enables us to make up for the backwards state of social-scientific functionalism in comparison to biocybernetics and to grasp goal states of social systems in a non-arbitrary way.[7] Normativistically employed systems analysis has a weak empirical content because it can only chance upon causally effective mechanisms from arbitrarily chosen functional points of reference.

Its analytical limitedness is grounded in the circumstance that it cannot distinguish between *systematic* selectivity of an institutional system on the one hand, and merely accidental non-fulfillment of given norms (which could be fulfilled while retaining the selective structures) on the other (p. 86).

The remaining strategies mentioned by Offe are on another level. They can be understood as the search for empirical indicators of suppressed interests.

—One can proceed *immanently* in playing off "claim" and "reality" against one another. This method is commonly employed in the critical literature on constitutional law (constitutional claim versus constitutional reality). It carries with it, however, the burden of proof for the thesis that there is not merely a tendency for the unactualized claim to which the critique refers to be violated, but that this violation is systematic (p. 88).

—One can identify *rules of exclusion* codified in a political system—perhaps in the form of procedural rules of administrative law, civil laws, and penal laws. Such a procedure for analyzing structural selectivity is inadequate in so far as it can hardly be supposed that a social system itself designates in codified form the totality of restrictions effective within it (p. 88).

—A further possibility would be confronting political-administrative processes not with their own or with constitutional pretensions . . . but with the *unintended,* yet *systematically arising* "misunderstandings" and *over-interpretations* which they evoke (p. 89).

(One should not, of course, rely on the political system's making rejected claims sufficiently evident at all times.)

—Finally, one can adopt comparative procedures, identifying the rules of exclusion which distinguish one political system from another with the help of a *ceteris paribus* clause. . . . [But], for one thing, those selectivities which are common to the systems compared do not come into view; for another, conditions which would justify a rigorous application of the *ceteris paribus* clause are scarcely ever met with (p. 87).

These shortcomings in the search for indicators are trivial as long as the theoretical concept for which indicators are sought is lacking. Observed discrepancy between legal norms and legal reality, codified rules of exclusion, discrepancy between actual level of claims and politically permitted level of satisfaction, repressions that become visible in international comparison—all of these phenomena have the same status as other conflict phenomena: they can be called upon in crisis analysis only if they can be ordered in a theoretical system for description and evaluation. A version of the advocacy model based on principles presents itself for this purpose. I do not mean by this the empirical feedback of critique on the goals of conflict groups—goals that are chosen on the basis of pre-theoretical experiences, that is, with partisanship. For the latter formulation would render partisanship immune to demands for foundations. Instead, the advocacy role of the critical theory of society would consist in ascertaining generalizable, though nevertheless suppressed, interests in a representatively simulated discourse between groups that are differentiated (or could be non-arbitrarily differentiated) from one another by articulated, or at least virtual, opposition of interests. A discourse carried through as advocacy can lead only to a hypothetical result.[8] But pointed indicators for testing such hypotheses can be sought in the abovementioned dimensions with some hope of success.

Chapter 4. The End of the Individual?

I have sought to prove that practical questions *can* be treated discursively and that it is *possible* for social-scientific analysis to take the relation of norm systems to truth methodically into consideration. It is an open question whether in complex societies motive formation is *actually* still tied to norms that require justification, or whether norm systems have lost their relation to truth.

The previous course of human history confirms the anthropologically informed view of Durkheim, who always conceived *society* as a *moral reality*. Classical sociology never doubted that subjects capable of speaking and acting could develop the unity of their person only in connection with identity-securing world-views and moral systems. The unity of the person requires the unity-enhancing perspective of a life-world that guarantees order and has both cognitive and moral-practical significance.

> The most important function of society is nomization. The anthropological presupposition for this is a human craving for meaning that appears to have the force of instinct. Men are congenitally compelled to impose a meaningful order upon reality. This order, however, presupposes the social enterprise of ordering world-construction. To be separated from society exposes the individual to a multiplicity of dangers with which he is unable to cope by himself, in the extreme case to the danger of immanent extinction. Separation from society also inflicts unbearable psychological tensions upon the individual, tensions that are grounded in the root anthropological fact of sociality. The ultimate danger of such separation, however, is the danger of meaninglessness. This danger is the nightmare par excellence, in which the individual is submerged in a world of disorder, senselessness and madness. Reality and identity are malignantly transformed into meaningless figures of horror. To be in society is to be "sane" precisely in the sense of being shielded from the ultimate "insanity" of such anomic terror. Anomie is unbearable to the point where the individual may seek death in preference to it. Conversely, existence within a nomic world may be sought at the cost of all sorts of sacrifice and suffering—and even at the cost of life itself, if the individual believes that this ultimate sacrifice has nomic significance.[1]

The fundamental function of world-maintaining interpretive systems is the avoidance of chaos, that is, the overcoming of contingency. The legitimation of orders of authority and basic norms can be understood as a specialization of this "meaning-giving" function. Religious systems originally connected the moral-practical task of constituting ego- and group-identities (differentiation of the ego *vis-à-vis* the social-reference group on the one hand, and differentiation of the collective *vis-à-vis* the natural and social environment on the other) with the cognitive interpretation of the world (mastery of problems of survival that arise in the confrontation with outer nature) in such a way that the contingencies of an imperfectly controlled environment could be processed simultaneously with the fundamental risks of human existence. I am thinking here of crises of the life-cycle and the dangers of socialization, as well as of injuries to moral and physical integrity (guilt and loneliness, sickness and death). The "meaning" promised by religion has always been ambivalent. On the one hand, by promising meaning, it preserved the claim—until now constitutive for the socio-cultural form of life—that men ought not to be satisfied with fictions but only with "truths" when they wish to know why something happens in the way it does, how it happens, and how what they do and ought to do can be justified. On the other hand, promise of meaning has always implied a promise of consolation as well, for proffered interpretations do not simply bring the unsettling contingencies to consciousness but make them bearable as well—even when, and precisely when, they cannot be removed *as* contingencies.

In primitive stages of social development, the problems of survival—and thus man's experiences of contingency in dealing with outer nature—were so drastic that they had to be counterbalanced by the narrative production of an illusion of order, as can be clearly seen in the content of myth.[2] With increased control over outer nature, secular knowledge became independent of worldviews, which were increasingly restricted to functions of social integration. The sciences eventually established a monopoly on the interpretation of outer nature; they devalued inherited global interpretations and transformed the mode of faith into a scientistic attitude that permits only faith in the objectivating sciences. In this domain, contingencies are recognized and, to a large extent, technically mastered and their consequences made bearable. Natural catastrophes are defined as world-wide social events [*Sozialfälle*], and their effects are blunted by large-scale administrative operations. (Interestingly, the consequences of war belong in this category of administered humanity.) On the other hand, with growing complexity in areas of social co-existence, a number of new contingencies have been produced, without a proportionate growth in the ability to master contingencies. Hence, the need for interpretations that overcome contingency and divest not-yet-controlled accidents of their accidental character no longer arises in relation to outer nature; but it is regenerated in an intensified form by suffering from uncontrolled societal processes. Today the social sciences can no longer take on the functions of world-views. Instead, at the same time that they dissolve the metaphysical illusion of order last produced by the objectivistic philosophy of history, they contribute to an increase in avoidable contingencies; for in their present state they do not produce technical knowledge that society could use for mastering contingency; nor do they have confidence in the ability of strong theoretical strategies to penetrate the multiplicity of *apparent,* nominalistically produced contingencies and make the objective context of social evolution accessible. Considering the risks to individual life that exist, a theory that could interpret away the facticities of loneliness and guilt, sickness and death is, to be sure, not even *conceivable.* Contingencies that are irremovably attached to the bodily and moral constitution of the individual can be raised to consciousness only *as* contingency. We must, in principle, live disconsolately with them.

Moreover, to the extent that world-views are impoverished, morality too is formalized and detached from substantive interpretations. Practical reason can no longer be founded in the transcendental subject. Communicative ethics appeals now only to fundamental norms of rational speech, an ultimate "fact of reason." Of course, if this is taken to be a simple fact, capable of no further explanation, it is not possible to see why there should still issue from it a normative force that organizes the self-understanding of men and orients their action.

At this point we can return to the question with which we began. If world-views have foundered on the separation of cognitive from socially integrative components, if world-maintaining interpretive systems today belong irretrievably to the past, then what fulfills the moral-practical task of constituting ego- and group-identity? Could a universalistic linguistic ethics no longer connected to cognitive interpretations of nature and society (*a*) adequately stabilize itself, and (*b*) structurally secure the identities of individuals and collectives in the framework of a world society? Or is a universal morality without cognitive roots condemned to shrink to a grandiose tautology in which a claim to reason overtaken by evolution now merely opposes the empty affirmation of itself to the objectivistic self-understanding of men? Have changes in the mode of socialization that affect the socio-cultural form of life perhaps already come about under the rhetorical guise of a universalistic morality that has lost its force? Does the new universal language of systems theory indicate that the "avant garde" have already begun the retreat to particular identities, settling down in the unplanned, nature-like system of world society like the Indians on the reservations of contemporary America? Finally, would such a definitive withdrawal mean the renunciation of the immanent relation of motive-shaping norms to truth?

An affirmative answer to these questions cannot as yet be sufficiently justified with a reference to the developmental logic of world-views. For, in the first place, the repoliticization of the biblical inheritance observable in contemporary theological discussion (Pannenberg, Moltmann, Solle, Metz),[3] which goes together with a leveling of this-worldly/other-worldly dichotomy, does not mean atheism in the sense of a liquidation without trace of the idea of God—although the idea of a *personal* God would hardly seem to be salvageable with consistency from *this* critical mass of thought. The idea of God is transformed [*aufgehoben*] into the concept of a *Logos* that determines the community of believers and the real life-context of a self-emancipating society. "God" becomes the name for a communicative structure that forces men, on pain of a loss of their humanity, to go beyond their accidental, empirical nature to encounter one another *indirectly*, that is, across an objective something that they themselves are not.

Secondly, it has in no way been determined that the philosophical impulse to conceive of a demythologized unity of the world cannot also be retained through scientific argumentation. Science can certainly not take over the functions of world-views. But general theories (whether of social development or of nature)[4] contradict consistent scientific thought less than its positivistic self-misunderstanding. Like the irrecoverably criticized world-views, such theoretical strategies also hold the promise of meaning: the overcoming of contingencies. But, at the same time, they aim at methodically removing from this promise the ambivalence between truth claim and a merely illusory fulfillment. We can no longer avert recognizable contingencies by producing a rationalizing illusion.

The fact that the developmental logic of world-views *does not exclude* the continuance of a mode of socialization related to·truth may be comforting. Nevertheless, the steering imperatives of highly complex societies could necessitate disconnecting the formation of motives from norms capable of justification and setting aside, as it were, of the detached superstructure of normative structures. If this happened, legitimation problems *per se* would cease to exist. A number of reflections from the history of ideas [*geistesgeschicht-lichen*] speak for this tendency. I would like to draw attention to them with a few catchphrases.

a) For more than a hundred years, it has been possible to observe the cynicism of a, as it were, self-denying bourgeois consciousness —in philosophy, in a consciousness of the times determined by cultural pessimism, and in political theory. Nietzsche radicalized the experience of the retrenchment of the ideas with which reality could be confronted: "For why has the advent of nihilism become necessary? Because the values we have had hitherto thus draw their final consequence; because nihilism represents the ultimate logical conclusion of our great values and ideas—because we must experience nihilism before we can find out what value these 'values' really had." [5] Nietzsche assimilated the historical loss of force of normative validity claims as well as the Darwinian impulses to a naturalistic self-destruction of reason. He replaced the question: "How are synthetic judgments *a priori* possible?" with another: "Why is the belief in such judgments necessary?" "Valuations" take the place of "truths." Theory of knowledge is replaced by a perspectival theory of the affects whose highest principle is "that every belief, every taking-for-true, is necessarily false because there is no true world." [6] Nietzsche counted on the shock effect of his revelations; and his heroic style also reveals the pain that cutting the umbilical cord to the universalism of the Enlightenment caused him after all. This ambivalence was echoed in the Nietzsche reception of the twenties, down to Gottfried Benn, Carl Schmitt, Ernst Junger, and Arnold Gehlen. Today the pain has either been reduced to nostalgia or given way to a new innocence—if not precisely to the innocence that Nietzsche once postulated—for which positivism and existentialism have prepared the foundations.

Anyone who still discusses the admissibility of truth in practical questions is, at best, old-fashioned.

b) The revocation of bourgeois ideals can be seen with particular clarity in the retrograde development of democratic theory (which was from the start, of course, presented in both a radical version and a version leading to liberalism).[7] In reaction to the Marxist critique of bourgeois democracy, Mosca, Pareto and Michels introduced the elite theory of domination as the realistic, scientific antidote to natural-law idealism. Schumpeter and Max Weber gathered these elements into a theory of mass democracy. In their sober pathos is still reflected the sacrifice that a purportedly better insight into a pessimistic anthropology seems to demand. A new generation of outspoken elite theorists already stands beyond cynicism and self-pity. They adopt Tocqueville as an honorable precursor and recommend the new elitism in good conscience as the simple alternative to the dark night of totalitarianism in which all cats are grey. Peter Bachrach has demonstrated an interesting shrinking process in the "theory of democratic rule by elites" as it is presented by authors like Kornhauser, Lipset, Truman, and Dahrendorf.[8] Democracy, in this view, is no longer determined by the content of a form of life that takes into account the generalizable interests of all individuals. It counts now as only a method for selecting leaders and the accoutrements of leadership. Under "democracy," the conditions under which all legitimate interests can be fulfilled by way of realizing the fundamental interest in self-determination and participation are no longer understood. It is now only a key for the distribution of rewards conforming to the system, that is, a regulator for the satisfaction of private interests. This democracy makes possible *prosperity without freedom*. It is no longer tied to political equality in the sense of an equal distribution of political power, that is, of the chances to exercise power. Political equality now means only the formal right to equal opportunity of *access* to power, that is, "equal eligibility for election to positions of power." Democracy no longer has the goal of rationalizing authority through the participation of citizens in discursive processes of will-formation. It is intended, instead, to make possible *compromises* between ruling elites. Thus, the substance of classical democratic theory is finally surrendered. No longer *all* politically consequential decisions, but only those decisions of the government still *defined as political*, are to be subject to the precepts of democratic will-formation. In this way, a pluralism of elites, replacing the self-determination of the people, makes privately exercised social power independent of the pressures of legitimation and immunizes it against the principle of rational formation of will. According to the new theory of authority, the presuppositions of democracy are fulfilled

> if (a) the voters can choose between competing elites; (b) the elites do not succeed in making their power hereditary or in blocking the access of new social groups to elite positions; (c) the elites are dependent on the support of shifting coalitions, so that no exclusive form of domination can take over; and (d) the elites which dominate in different social spheres—for example, in business, education and art—can form no common alliance.[9]

c) In all the many symptoms of a destruction of practical reason to be found in the history of ideas—of which I have indicated a few examples—there is expressed a change of position in bourgeois consciousness, which allows of different interpretations. Either we are dealing with a class-specific phenomena of retreat from universalistic demands, claims to autonomy, and expectations of authenticity, that endanger the class compromise in advanced capitalism as soon as they are sued for; or we have to do with a general movement against a culture that has prevailed, in the absence of alternatives (but has become universal in spite of its bourgeois origins), against a form of life fundamental to the history of the species, in which the logic of social reproduction works through norms that admit of truth. The radical interpretation, which sees the mode of socialization of the species placed in question, can be formulated as the thesis of the "end of the individual."

Michael Landmann's pithy statement, "The three millennia of the individual have come to a close," [10] can still be understood as an offshoot of a cultural critique that sees only a certain historical formation of the human spirit perishing with the old Europe. But I am thinking here of those more relentless interpretations that diagnose the death of the form of the bourgeois individual: in this view, the reproduction of highly complex societies necessitates *a transposition at the level of their previous constituents.* With the historical form of the bourgeois individual, there appeared those (still unfulfilled) claims to autonomous ego-organization within the framework of an independent—that is, rationally founded—practice. In these claims was laid out the logic of a general (if undeveloped, nevertheless continuously effective) socialization [*Vergesellschaftung*] through individuation. If this form of reproduction were to be surrendered, together with the imperatives logically embedded in it, the social system could no longer establish its unity through formation of the identities of socially related individuals. The constellations of general and particular would no longer be relevant for the aggregate state of the society.

Horkheimer and Adorno develop this idea as a "dialectic of enlightenment," which Albrecht Wellmer summarizes as follows:

> The external destiny in which men had to become involved for the sake of emancipation from their slavery to nature is at the same time their inner destiny, a destiny which reason suffers at its own hands. In the end, the subjects for whose sake the subjection, reification, and disenchantment of nature were begun are themselves so repressed, reified, and disenchanted in their own eyes, that even their efforts at emancipation result in the opposite—in fortifying the context of delusion in which they are caught. With the overthrow of the animistic world-view, the dialectic of enlightenment had already begun, a dialectic which, in capitalist industrial society, has been driven to the point where "even man has become an anthropomorphism in the eyes of man." [11]

This diagnosis agrees—not in its foundation but in its substance—with that of Gehlen and Schelsky. Schelsky's reflection on the self-interpretation of man in scientific civilization leads to the conclusion that the "scientific-technical process of creation" induces a "total cutting off of previous history" and a "change in the identity of man."

> This reflection on "man" is more than merely the moral-ideological reflex of the technical-scientific self-production of man. It is the

documentation of a new self-estrangement of man which came into the world with the new scientific civilization. The danger that the creator is losing himself in his work, the constructor losing himself in his construction, is now the metaphysical temptation of man. Man shrinks back from transferring himself without remainder into self-produced objectivity, into a constructed being, and yet works unceasingly at the continuation of the process of scientific-technical self-objectivation. Whereas man had first understood and deplored the rise of the rational, technical world of labor as a split between himself and the world, as an alienation from an old "animate unity" with the world, the new unity of man with the world, which he has constructed and earned out of spirit, is now becoming a threat to the identity which man had gained precisely in that split. The endurance of the split—Hegel's final demand in the face of the "confusion of the age"—still made possible the identification of man with his old metaphysical subjectivity precisely because it "released" the latter from the world of the beginning labor society. Today that split is historically already vanishing, and the metaphysical homelessness which obtrudes from the new world/man unity is documented in a backwards-looking metaphysical longing, is fixated on the memory of the freedom of subjectivity in the split and alienation from the world.[12]

Schelsky, however, ceases to be consistent when he reverts (formerly, at any rate) to a standpoint transcending the sphere of society[13] and recommends "continuing metaphysical reflection" as a useful medium through which the threatened individual can escape the forces of objectivation and establish himself again beyond the "limits of the social."

> The continuous heightening of reflective consciousness in itself is induced precisely by the technical-scientific objectivation of the achievements of consciousness. It is the form in which the thinking subject strives to keep ahead of its own objectification, and thus assures itself of its superiority over its own world-process.[14]

Schelsky wrote these words ten years before the appearance of *Negative Dialectic*. They fit no one's existence better than Adorno's. But Adorno, more consistently than Schelsky, entertains no illusions about the death of the bourgeois individual. He sees, rather, even in the "institutionalization of continuing reflection," [15] a revaluation of individuality which simply masks its destruction. Under the heading *"Dummer August,"* Adorno remarks:

> It is still too optimistic to think that the individual is being altogether liquidated. If only it were true that in his conclusive negation, in the abolition of monads through solidarity, there was embedded at the same time the salvation of the individual being that would become a particular precisely only in its relation to the general! The present state of affairs is far removed from this. The disaster transpires not as the radical extinction of what has been, but because what has been historically condemned is dragged along—dead, neutralized, power-less—and pulls ignominiously downwards. In the midst of standard-ized and administered human units, the individual lives on. He is even placed under protection and gains monopoly value. But he is in truth merely the function of his own uniqueness, a showpiece like the deformed who were stared at with astonishment and mocked by children. Since he no longer leads an independent economic existence, his character falls into contradiction with his objective social role. Precisely for the sake of this contradiction, he is sheltered in a nature preserve, enjoyed in leisurely contemplation.[16]

Discussions about the splendor and the poverty of bourgeois subjectivity easily take on a non-binding character because after Hegel we are ill equipped to enter into the dimension of the history of consciousness. This becomes clear in the argumentation of Willms, who seeks to place himself between Gehlen and Luhmann, employing once again a Hegelian figure of thought.[17] He projects the identity-formation of the bourgeois individual onto the level of international relations and equates the splendor of the bourgeois subject with the world-historical generality of an imperialistic power position (of the USA and Europe) that is today being relativized by China and the Third World. The poverty of the bourgeois subject consists, then, in his uncomprehended particular-ity. If one reads the Hegelian philosophy of right with the eyes of Carl Schmitt, this can be valid. But one has to pose the question of whether the formal structures of linguistic ethics, in which bourgeois humanism interpreted itself from Kant to Hegel and Marx, reflect *nothing* more than a decisionistic presumption of a monopoly on the definition of humanity—"the history of bourgeois society is the history of those who define who man is"—or whether it is not rather the case that this reduction itself represents one of the long-finished and meanwhile arbitrary melodies of bourgeois self-mutilation to which Adorno attests: "there remains from the critique of bourgeois consciousness only that shrug of the shoulders with which all physicians have manifested their secret understanding with death." [18]

d) Until now no one has succeeded in extracting the thesis of the end of the individual from the domain of the malaise and self-experience of intellectuals and made it accessible to empirical test. But subjectivity is not an interior something; for the reflexivity of the person grows in proportion to his externalization. The identity of the ego is a symbolic structure which, with the growing complexity of society, must remove itself centrifugally further and further from its middle point in order to stabilize itself. The person exposes himself to more and more contingencies; he is thrust further and further into an ever-tighter net of reciprocal defenselessness and exposed needs for protection. Thus, since Marx, those socio-structural limitations that restrict the process of individuation and deform the structure of being-with-oneself-in-being-outside-of-oneself [*Ausser-sich-bei-sich-Seins*] (that is, which disturb the precarious balance between externalization and appropriation), has been analyzed under the title of "alienation." "Alienation" has, in the meantime, become the catchword for *a direction in social psychological research.*[19]

Etzioni interprets alienation as "unresponsiveness of the world to the actor, which subjects him to forces he neither comprehends nor guides." [20] He distinguishes from this a hidden form of alienation—namely, "inauthenticity"—which has, of course, different connotations in the German-speaking world than in the French-speaking world. "A relationship, institution or society is inauthentic if it provides the appearance of responsiveness while the underlying condition is alienating." [21] This differentiation takes account, firstly, of the fact that in advanced-capitalist societies phenomena of alienation have been detached from manifestations of pauperism. But, above all, this distinction takes account of the remarkable integrative power and elasticity of this society. These qualities are expressed in the fact that social conflicts can be shifted to the level of psychic problems, that they can be charged to individuals as private matters; and in the fact that mental conflicts that are repoliticized as protest can be shunted aside, made into problems that can be administratively treated, and institutionalized as proof of the extended scope of tolerance. The student protest of recent years provides a good illustration of this mechanism. The essential impulse is directed against the anticipated strategies of absorption; these are supposed to be undermined by imaginative provocations. But by and large this has not succeeded. Instead of releasing the normative power of institutions in the form of open repression (which has *also* happened), the degree of tolerance has increased. The headlines already report on university strikes and citizens' initiatives, regretfully adding "without incident." The new techniques of demonstration have altered little but the level of expectation. Thus there arises a gray area in which the social system can live with the non- (or not-yet-) institutionalized opposition it calls forth without having to solve the problems that are the occasion, ground, or cause of the protests. Blows directed against stonewalls bounce off rubber screens.

This metaphorical localization of a domain of phenomena explains nothing. At best, it illustrates that phenomena of alienation are being increasingly replaced by manifestations of inauthenticity. Above all, it is unclear how we are to interpret the inauthenticity whose traces Etzioni pursues in the system of social labor, in the public domain of politics, and in the personality system itself.[22] Are we dealing with reactions, uncontrollable in the long run, against the continued violation of normative structures that are at odds with the growing steering needs of the political-economic system? Or are we dealing with the birth pangs of a fundamentally new mode of socialization? It could indeed be the case that both tendencies—the politically released and stimulated social eudaemonism that can be understood according to principles of a strategic-utilitarian ethics, as well as the politically blunted, subculturally released pleonexy that comes to terms with the program of immediate satisfaction in expanded scopes of contingency—find a common denominator in their renunciation of the justification of practice on the basis of norms that admit of truth.

Since I cannot see how this question can be directly decided empirically, I would like to examine it indirectly with the help of Luhmann's theory, which proceeds from the *undiscussed presupposition* that the creation of motivation needed by the system is in no way restricted today by independent [*eigensinnigen*] systems of norms that follow a logic of their own, but responds to steering imperatives alone.

Chapter 5. Complexity and Democracy

Luhmann regards a communication theory that analyzes legitimation problems with reference to the discursive redemption of normative-validity claims as "out of step with social reality." [1] He chooses for his initial problem, not the foundation of norms and opinions, that is, the constitution of a rational practice, but the selection pressure of complex systems of action in a world that is contingent, that is, that could also be otherwise.

> Habermas sees the subject, just as the intersubjectivity which precedes it, primarily as a potential for foundations admitting of truth. The subjectivity of man consists for him in the possibility of specifying rational grounds in intersubjective communication, or of being able to accommodate oneself to such grounds or to the refutation of one's own grounds. He thereby captures, however, only a derivative aspect—and, moreover, one which seems to me to be historically conditioned and long antiquated—of a much more deeply seated concept of the subject. [2]

According to Luhmann, the attempt "to tie the inherited claim of Western humanity which bears the title of 'reason' to such a concept of the subject" leads necessarily to a systematic underestimation of the problem of world complexity. "The subject must first be thought of as contingent selectivity." [3] Problems of domination and distribution that are posed from the point of view of the class structure of society have become obsolete. [4] They betray an "old European" perspective in which genuine problems, which appear from the point of view of ranges of alternatives and capacities for decision, are concealed.

"Almost everything could be possible, and I can change almost nothing." This sentence expresses Luhmann's fundamental experience. It *could* be interpreted to mean that, on the one hand, highly complex class societies have, because of their potential for productivity, considerably extended the range of possibilities for controlling the environment and organizing themselves; or that, on the other hand, due to their unplanned, nature-like principle of organization, they are subject to limitations that prevent autonomous utilization of the abstract possibilities and result, moreover, in an excess of self-produced (avoidable) environmental complexity.[5] In fact, however, Luhmann interprets his experience in the contrary sense: that, with its drastically extended scope of contingency, the social system acquires degrees of freedom which place it under increased pressure of problems and decisions. The structures and states of complex social systems have, at least in the domain of organization and politics, become non-essential [*zufällig*] and thus capable of being practically chosen; but how to decide among alternatives opened up now is a problem that relativizes all others. After Luhmann has distinguished between determinate and indeterminate complexity of system and environment,[6] the real problem of reduction is no longer the (indeterminate) complexity of the environment. It is rather environmental complexity made determinable by environmental projects relative to the system, that is, the self-overloading of the system with its own capacities for problem resolution. Highly complex social systems must wear themselves out on problems resulting from their growing autonomy, that is, on necessities resulting from their freedom.

As soon as the priority of this problem is established, further steps follow automatically. The problem of world complexity requires an essentialistic and exclusive application of the concept of system. A number of important points follow from this.

1) Complex societies are no longer held together and integrated through normative structures. Their unity is no longer established intersubjectively through communications penetrating the minds of socially related individuals. System integration, treated from a steering perspective, becomes independent of a social integration accessible from life-world perspectives.

2) Man's understanding of self and of the world, detached from

system identity, slips into provincialism to the extent that it remains "old European," that is, oriented to normative claims; or it detaches itself altogether from norm orientations and brings the consciousness of the individual into the same situation as the system; he learns "to project and endure an infinitely open, in the final analysis ontically indeterminate, contingent world and to use it as the basis of all selective experience and action."[7]

3) The reproduction of highly complex societies depends on the differentiated steering system, on the political subsystem. By increasing its capacity to process information and its indifference to other social subsystems, the political system acquires a unique autonomy within the society.

> Politics can no longer presuppose its decision basis, but must itself create it. It must accomplish its own legitimation in a situation which is defined as open and structurally indeterminate with respect to the chances of consensus and to the results striven for.[8]

Separating the legitimation system from the administration makes possible the autonomy of decision processes *vis-à-vis* the input of generalized motivations, values, and interests.

4) Since the social system can no longer constitute a world that stamps the identity of subsystems,[9] the functions of politics can no longer be understood with a glance at the "correct" policy demanded of the administrative system by society.

> Reduced to a brief formula, it has to do with the fact that the political system can no longer derive its identity from the society if it is required by the society precisely as a contingent system which could possibly be otherwise. It must, then, identify itself through structural selection in a situation of consciousness no longer comprehensible with old European concepts.[10]

Under these conditions it is meaningless to want to increase the reflexivity of the administration by tying it to the society through discursive will-formation and participation.

> Decision processes are . . . processes of eliminating other possibilities. They produce more "nays" than "yeas," and the more rationally

they proceed, the more extensively they test other possibilities, the greater becomes their rate of negation. To demand an intensive, engaged participation of all in them would be to make a principle of frustration. Anyone who understands democracy in this way has, in fact, to come to the conclusion that it is incompatible with rationality.[11]

5) The new systems-theoretic approach brings with it a new linguistic system, claiming universality, that is interpreted *vis-à-vis* competing approaches through a transformation of fundamental classical concepts (such as politics, authority, legitimacy, power, democracy, public opinion, etc.).[12] Each of these systems-theoretic translations is also a critique of the unsuitability of "old European" concept formation, which has become obsolete with the evolutionary step to post-modern society. Because the problem of world complexity has assumed the leading position, the problem of a rational organization of society in conjunction with formation of motives through norms that admit of truth has lost its object.

The unwieldy problem of the relation between *complexity and democracy* can be most easily formulated in a workable manner at the level of planning theory. Planning discussion in the last ten years has,[13] among other things, led to two opposed types of politics in which are expressed two styles of planning: on the one hand, pluralistic-incrementalist process politics, which limits itself mainly to conditional planning, and, on the other, rational-comprehensive systems politics, which requires mainly program planning.[14] These types can be understood as the respective end points of a scale on which patterns of action and reaction of planning bureaucracies can be delineated. If we add a further dimension, namely participation by members of the social system who are affected by planning, the following types of politics result.

Participation of those affected	Planning Style	
	Incrementalist	Comprehensive
Not permitted	A	B
Permitted	C	D

"Participation" here means a general taking part, on the basis of equal opportunity, in discursive processes of will-formation. According to this definition, Type-C politics would exclude usual strategies for attenuating and avoiding conflict that are characteristic of pluralistic Type A: bracketing controversial goals and values and restriction of the negotiation process to the purposive-rational realization of goals that admit of consensus; making obligatory negotiation procedures formalistically independent of their contents; carefully segmenting the areas of planning; and so on.[15] Analogously, Type-D politics is incompatible with technocratic retreats into a pretended sphere of objective forces [*Sachzwängen*] in which political questions are interpreted as technical questions and specialists are immunized against the latent or suppressed dissent of those affected that is characteristic of the conflict-avoidance behavior of Type B.

Luhmann's planning theory marks out one of these types of politics as appropriate for complex societies, namely, comprehensive, non-participatory planning (B). This does not come in the form of a practical recommendation. Rather, Luhmann believes he can show that the reproduction of highly complex societies leaves no choice but that of anchoring the required reflexivity of society in an administrative system shielded from parties and the public, instead of in a democratically organized public domain. "We can speak of the politicization of administration . . . to the extent that the administration itself reflects on its position in the political system of society and identifies itself accordingly as contingent, as possibly otherwise." [16] This thesis is based on (*a*) a description of the interaction between the administration and the other subsystems of society, (*b*) a causal hypothesis about the observable restrictions on administrative planning capacity, and (*c*) a fundamental assumption regarding the theory of social evolution.

Re *a*) In complex societies, a control center has been differentiated as an administrative system and has, according to Luhmann, assumed the commanding position *vis-à-vis* the other social subsystems. The autonomous administration has general competency to deal with all steering problems that remain unsettled in the society. It is competent not only in the sense of responsibility, but also in its ability to solve problems. Since there are no structures in the society not, in the last analysis, at the disposition of the administration, there is no class of problems whose solution would, in principle, force the administration to confront the limits of its capacity. In his description, Luhmann is generalizing experiences from which strikingly adaptive mechanisms of advanced capitalist societies can indeed be inferred.

On the other hand, there is also sufficient evidence of the limits of administrative planning capacity, which turn up again and again in an *ad hoc* manner, and of the merely reactive form of motion of a bureaucracy that withdraws into avoidance strategies. A politico-economic planning theory that interprets these experiences as crisis management comes to the contrary view that the administrative system is dependent on its environment, especially on the inherent dynamics of the economic system. I have sharpened this thesis by viewing the scope of action of the administrative system as limited on *two* sides: in steering the economic sector, by the parameters of a property order that it cannot change; in creating motivation, by the independent [*eigensinnig*] development of normative structures that are irreconcilable with the suppression of generalizable interests.

Re *b*) The two competing descriptions, which emphasize either the autonomy or the dependency of the state apparatus, can be weighed by arguments that achieve, at best, a certain plausibility.[17] But the manner in which one explains the easily observable restrictions on the administrative system's planning capacity depends on which description one adopts. Luhmann traces rationality deficits to the fact that administration has not yet become sufficiently independent of politics.

> The chances for that separation of politics from administration lie in a heightening of selection performance, above all in the possibility of varying the premises of administrative action—such as organization, personnel and programs—from political perspectives in the narrower sense, without the variation of structures impairing their structuring function . . . The administration's possession of its own structure means that it has its own possibilities, which need not be

identical with the expectations of the environment; and non-identity
with the environment even at the level of possibilities gives the
opportunity for self-steering. At the same time, with this separation
even of the constitution of possibilities, the risk must be assumed
that the problems that the political system solves are not the
problems of the society.[18]

According to Luhmann, rationality deficits can be eliminated only
to the extent that the administration develops an identity independent of the society and understands itself as the authority responsible
for the expansion of the horizon of possibility and the collateral
thematization of alternatives excluded at that time. As long as the
administration remains dependent on inputs from the public
domain and party politics, on the one hand, and from those affected
and the interested clientele on the other, the self-reflection that
strengthens selectivity will be inhibited. Luhmann sees the vanishing point of the non-political differentiation of an administration
capable of comprehensive planning in a fusion of science and
administration that would, simultaneously, suspend the autonomy
of science and undifferentiate the previously separated media of
power and truth.

> Only the administration *itself* can investigate itself to an extent
> which could induce political reflection and contribute to reducing
> that reflection deficit (of the administration). In this sense, "politici-
> zation" amounts, in the final analysis, to linking scientific *self*-investi-
> gation to structural selection, a linkage that could place in question
> the classical differentiation of experience and action, knowledge and
> decision, truth and power.[19]

With this statement Luhmann expresses his version of the end of
the individual. The accelerated growth of complexity makes it
necessary for society to convert to a form of reproduction that gives
up the differentiation between power and truth in favor of a
nature-like development withdrawn from reflection.[20]

At the moment I can see three competing explanations. In the
first, in contrast to Luhmann, F. Naschold traces the bottleneck in
administrative planning to too great an independence of the
administration from political will-formation. He believes that

political steering capacity can be increased only through expanded participation in planning by those affected.[21] The "adaptation of political steering processes to society" is the only option still open for releasing previously unused resources and energies. (Of course, there is a risk that the extent of participation processes cannot be adequately controlled.) Naschold considers the multifunctional employment of participatory planning, which can serve to manipulate mass loyalty, improve information (by providing early warning and aiding consideration of values), and ease the burdens of the bureaucracy (through self-help organizations). These functions of apparent participation [*Scheinpartizipation*] do expand the administration's control over its environment. But it is not altogether clear whether Naschold believes that participation, in my sense of taking part in discursive will-formation, also signifies a "productive force for heightening the inherent variety of the political system." He does speak of "participation as a means for finding individual and collective identities, and of self-organizability as one precondition for taking part in a pluralistic politics of distribution." [22]

As set forth above (Part II, Chapter 5), Offe defends the view that the contradictory steering imperatives of the economic system represent an insuperable limit to rationality for the state in advanced capitalism. The adaptation of political steering processes to society, in the sense of rigorously prepared participatory planning, would remove bottlenecks in administrative planning because it would put an end to those selective class structures that cause cumulative production of avoidable environmental complexity.

Finally, Scharpf is aware of those restrictions that the inherent dynamics of the economic system impose on the state in advanced capitalism. But even a politics unburdened of these restrictions "would be surprised by unforeseen developments, overtaken by the unanticipated consequences of its measures, and frustrated by the counterintuitive results of its planning, if the capacity of its information and decision systems fell behind the requirements." [23] In contrast to Luhmann, Scharpf reckons with a limit to the increase in complexity that is immanent in administration. If one surmounts the segmented decision structure, which is unsuitable to an interdependent problem structure, in favor of comprehensive planning in centralized decision-structures, policy planning will rapidly arrive at a limit where its capacity for processing information and building consensus is overloaded by the excessive complexity of the problems (which are distinguished by high interdependency).

> Even if there were in the decision process no consolidated interests and resistance to change based on power potential . . . the attempt at simultaneous problematization and positively coordinated change of interdependent decision spheres must—beyond a narrowly drawn limit, which needs to be more precisely determined but is certainly disappointing—necessarily end in the frustration of total immobilism.[24]

Luhmann's assumption of an (in principle) unlimited extension of administrative steering capacity, which makes the administration independent of politics and—through incorporation of the scientific system—the locus of an eccentric self-reflection of society, can scarcely be supported with indicators from the experiential domain of political planning. In fact, systems-logical arguments support the view that participation that does not merely represent a concealed form of manipulation must limit rather than heighten administrative planning capacity. The rationalizing effect of "adapting political steering processes to society" is difficult to determine, for democratization would, on the one hand, dismantle the *avoidable* complexity (unavoidable only in relation to a specific system) that is produced by the uncontrolled, inherent dynamics of the economic process. But, at the same time, it would bring the *unavoidable* (*not* specific to a system) complexity of generalized discursive processes of will-formation into play. It is probable that the practical rationality of a goal state connected to generalizable interests costs more than it saves in terms of systems rationality. Of course, the balance does not have to be negative, if the limits to complexity, which according to Scharpf's reflections are built into administration, are reached very soon. In this case, *one* complexity that follows unavoidably from the logic of unrestrained communication would be overtaken, as it were, by another complexity, following as unavoidably from the logic of comprehensive planning.

Re: *c*) Luhmann's option for the type of non-participatory, global, system planning that is realized in a self-reflective administration removed from politics cannot, at the present stage of the planning discussion, be grounded with compelling arguments. Indeed, the empirical evidence that *today* can be marshalled speaks rather against Luhmann's option. In the end, Luhmann does not base his position on planning-theoretic investigations, but on a fundamental assumption about social evolution. In his opinion, problems of the reduction of environmental complexity and of the expansion of system complexity have the commanding position in social evolution, so that only steering capacity decides the level of development of a society. This is in no way a trivial assumption, for it could well be that an evolutionary step in the dimension of world-views ʻand moral systems has to be paid for with an undifferentiation of the steering system; above all, it may be that it can be paid for without risk, that is, without endangering the (altered) continuity of the system. Luhmann does not, as far as I can see, thematize his assumption. Rather, he prejudges it by the choice of his methodological approach.

The choice of a concept of rationality is decisive for the structure of a planning theory. Planning theories conceived *in decision-theoretic terms* [*entscheidungslogisch*] are based on a concept of *the rationality of action* that is taken from the paradigm of purposive-rational choice of alternative means. The model of rational action is suited to theories of rational choice and to planning techniques in areas of strategic action. The limits of the model can be seen, however, in the attempt to develop empirically substantive theories of social systems. The theoretical strategy of choosing the concept of subjective rationality of action means a prior decision for normativistic approaches and for methodological individualism.[25]

Planning theories laid out *in systems-theoretic terms* are based on a concept of objective rationality that is taken from the paradigm of self-regulated systems. The pattern of *systems rationality* is suited for empirically substantive theories about object domains in which unities that are clearly demarcated from their environment can be identified. Then (but only then) stability or instability can be determined on the basis of a systems maintenance accessible to experience. Since the persistence of societies or of social subsystems cannot up to now be unproblematically ascertained, the theoretical strategy of choosing the concept of systems rationality results in a decision between (at least) three alternatives: first, to proceed normativistically, that is, to set the limits and goal states of the social systems investigated (examples of this can be found in the research practice of the sociology of organizations,[26] but Etzioni's concept of an "active society," which is based on postulated fundamental needs, also belongs in this class);[27] second, to proceed radically functionalistically, that is, to search for functional equivalents in a given context from arbitrarily varied points of reference (Luhmann); or, finally, to make the social-scientific application of systems theory dependent on a required theory of social evolution that allows non-conventional determination of levels of development and, therewith, of the limit values of system alterations that threaten identity.[28]

Finally, planning theories laid out in *communications-theoretic terms*[29] are based on a concept of *practical rationality* that can be gained from the paradigm of will-forming discourse (and which can be developed in the form of a consensus theory of truth). (I examined this model in Chapter 3, above.) It is suited to the critical investigation of constellations of interest that are at the basis of normative structures. This procedure of normative genesis must, of course, be connected to the systems-theoretic approach if it is to contribute to a suitable theory of social evolution.

With the choice of a concept of rationality, a prior decision as to the logical status of planning theory is made. Decision-theoretic planning theories are normative-analytic procedures, that is, techniques for planning. Systems-theoretic planning theories can likewise proceed normative-analytically. According to their level of aspiration, they amount either to technical planning aids or to normatively designed theories in which planning is understood as a political process. Luhmann's universal-functionalist planning theory, which also appears as a systems theory, is conceived as opportunistic in principle and undermines the opposition between empirical-analytic and normative-analytic modes of procedure. Its status can best be characterized as pragmatic: systems research itself is part of a life-process subject to the law of increasing selectivity and reducing complexity. A communicative planning theory also transcends this opposition, but for other reasons. In addition to descriptive statements about valid norms, on the one hand, and prescriptive statements that concern the choice of norms, on the other hand, it allows critically evaluative statements about the justifiability of (either existing or proposed) norms—that is, about the redeemability of normative-validity claims. Justifiable norms are like true sentences; they are neither facts nor values. The following schema sums up our discussion.

	Concepts of Rationality		
Status of the Theory	Purposive-rationality	Systems-rationality	Practical rationality
Empirical-analytic	———	biocybernetics	———
Normative-analytic	diverse planning techniques	theory of planning as a political process	———
Neither empirical-analytic nor normative-analytic	———	universal functionalism	critical theory of society

With the methodological choice between the universal-functionalist and the critical-reconstructive approaches, the question discussed in Part III of this essay is also implicitly decided: whether the reproduction of social life is still bound to reason and, especially, whether generation of motives is still bound to internalization of norms that have need of justification. If this is no longer the case, reconstruction of historically developed institutions and interpretive systems in accordance with a normative-genetic procedure has lost its object, and crisis theorems can no longer be constructed. Luhmann, of course, cannot allow a "rational" constitution of society in the above sense because systems theory, as a consequence of its conceptual strategy, integrates and subordinates itself to a fundamentally opportunistic life-process. However, *one* important argument speaks against the research strategy of Luhmann. While critical social theory can founder on a changed

reality, universal functionalism must suppose—that is, prejudge at
the analytical level—that this change in the mode of socialization
and the "end of the individual" have already come to pass.

Chapter 6.   *Partiality for Reason*

The fundamental question of the continued existence of a truth-dependent mode of socialization constitutive of society is, as one can
see, not easy to answer. This could lead one to think that it is not at
all a theoretically resoluble question, but a practical question:
should we rationally *desire* that social identity be formed through
the minds of socially related individuals or should it be sacrificed to
the problem—real or imagined—of complexity? To pose the
question *in this way* is, of course, to answer it. Whether the
constituents of a rational form of life should be retained cannot be
made the object of a rational will-formation that depends on those
very constituents. This requires, in any event, an appeal to the
partiality for reason. As partisanship, however, this partiality can be
justified only so long as alternatives are posed *within* an already
accustomed, shared communicative form of life. As soon as an
alternative appears that breaks this circuit of predecided intersubjectivity, the only universalizable partiality—the interest in
reason itself—becomes particular. Luhmann poses such an alternative: he subordinates, at the methodological level, all areas of
interaction steered through discursively redeemable validity claims
to systems-rational claims to power and increasing power. Such
monopolistic claims of an eccentric administration permit no
possibility of appeal; that is, they may not be measured against
standards of practical rationality, as was the case even in the
Leviathan.

   This perspective leads "old European" thought into temptation,
and not for the first time. One has already accepted his opponent's
point of view if one resigns before the difficulties of enlightenment,
and, with the goal of a rational organization of society, withdraws
into actionism—that is, if one makes a decisionistic start in the hope
that retrospectively, after the successful fact, justifications will be
found for the costs that have arisen.[1] Furthermore, the partiality for

reason just as little justifies the retreat to a Marxistically embel-
lished orthodoxy, which today can lead at best to the establishment
without argument of sheltered and politically ineffective subcul-
tures. Both paths are forbidden to a practice that binds itself to a
rational will, that is, that does not avoid demands for foundations,
but demands theoretical clarity about what we do *not* know. Even
if we could not know much more today than my argumentation
sketch suggests—and that is little enough—this circumstance
would not discourage critical attempts to expose the stress limits of
advanced capitalism to conspicuous tests; and it would most
certainly not paralyze the determination to take up the struggle
against the stabilization of a nature-like social system *over* the heads
of its citizens, that is, at the price of—so be it!—old European
human dignity.

Notes

Notes to Introduction

1. A number of the important contributions are collected in T. W. Adorno, *et al.*, *Der Positivismusstreit in der deutschen Soziologie* (Neuwied, 1969); cf. Habermas, *Zur Logik der Sozialwissenschaften* (Frankfurt, 1970).
2. K. O. Apel, *et al.*, *Hermeneutik und Ideologiekritik* (Frankfurt, 1971).
3. J. Habermas and Niklas Luhmann, *Theorie der Gesellschaft oder Sozialtechnologie?* (Frankfurt, 1971).
4. Many of the relevant publications appeared in the volumes mentioned in notes 2. and 3. above. Available in English are "On Systematically Distorted Communication" and "Towards a Theory of Communicative Competence," in *Inquiry*, *13* (1970): 205–18, 360–75; the Introduction to *Theory and Practice* (Boston, 1973), pp. 1–40; and the Postscript to *Knowledge and Human Interests*, in *Philosophy of the Social Sciences*, *3* (1973): 157–89. Cf. also T. McCarthy, "A Theory of Communicative Competence," in *Philosophy of the Social Sciences*, *3* (1973): 135–56.
5. Lichtheim, *From Marx to Hegel* (New York, 1971), pp. 175–76. The lines quoted originally appeared in a review of Habermas' *Erkenntnis und Interesse* (Frankfurt, 1968), which appeared in the *Times Literary Supplement*, June 5, 1969.
6. The Institute's progress report of April 1974, mentions, among others, projects on development and underdevelopment, economic crisis tendencies, political-administrative systems, alternatives in science, and potentials for conflict and withdrawal among youth.
7. Most of Horkheimer's essays are collected in *Kritische Theorie*, Alfred Schmidt, ed. 2 vols. (Frankfurt, 1968). A number of these appear in English translation in *Critical Theory* (New York, 1973). In what follows I shall be referring primarily to "Traditional and Critical Theory" (TCT) and "Zum Problem der Wahrheit" (PW). Several of Marcuse's *Zeitschrift* essays are collected in *Kultur und Gesellschaft, I* (Frankfurt, 1965). These have appeared in English translation in *Negations* (Boston, 1968).
8. Cf. R. Bubner, "Was ist kritische Theorie?" in *Hermeneutik und Ideologiekritik*, pp. 160–209; M. Theunissen, *Gesellschaft und Geschichte: Zur Kritik der kritischen Theorie* (Berlin, 1969).
9. Adorno, Horkheimer, *Dialektik der Aufklärung* (Amsterdam, 1947); English translation, *Dialectic of Enlightenment* (New York, 1972).
10. Cf. Marcuse's "The Affirmative Character of Culture," in *Negations*, pp. 88–133.
11. "Labor and Interaction: Remarks on Hegel's Jena *Philosophy of Mind*," in *Theory and Practice*, pp. 142–69; "Technology and Science as Ideology," in

Towards a Rational Society (Boston, 1970), pp. 81–122; *Knowledge and Human Interests* (Boston, 1971).

12. *Zur Logik der Sozialwissenschaften*, p. 220.

13. For the relevant publications, see note 4. above.

14. "Vorbereitende Bemerkungen zu einer Theorie der kommunikativen Kompetenz," in *Theorie der Gesellschaft oder Sozialtechnologie?*, pp. 101–41; p. 120.

15. Ibid., p. 120.

16. "Knowledge and Human Interests: A General Perspective," Appendix to *Knowledge and Human Interests*, pp. 301–17.

17. "Wahrheitstheorien," in *Wirklichkeit und Reflexion: Festschrift für Walter Schulz* (Pfullingen, 1973), pp. 211–65; p. 218. I have translated *begründen* here and in the text of the book as "justify." This has, perhaps, connotations in English that it need not have in German, as Karl Popper and his followers have equated justification with deductive proof and attacked it as an unattainable goal even for the natural sciences. But, as will be seen in Part III, Chapter 2 of the present volume, Habermas rejects this identification. As he employs the term, *Begründung* is a matter of providing good grounds or reasons *(Gründe)* for a claim; it is a pragmatic rather than a syntactical notion.

18. Ibid., pp. 239–40.

19. I have translated *rational motivieren* here and in the text as "provide rational grounds for," since "motivate" has predominantly psychological connotations in English, whereas *motivieren* can also be used in the sense of *begründen*.

20. "Wahrheitstheorien," p. 258.

21. Ibid., p. 259.

22. *Writings of the Young Marx on Philosophy and Society*, L. Easton and K. Guddat, eds. (Garden City, New York, 1967), p. 400.

23. Maurice Dobb, ed. (New York, 1970), pp. 20–21.

24. Cf. J. Habermas, *Knowledge and Human Interests*, Chaps. 2 and 3; cf. also A. Wellmer, *Critical Theory of Society* (New York, 1971) and "Communication and Emancipation: Reflections on the 'Linguistic Turn' in Critical Theory," in *Philosophy and Social Theory*, (State University of New York at) *Stony Brook Studies in Philosophy*, Vol. I (1974), pp. 75–101.

25. J. Habermas, *Toward a Rational Society*, p. 112.

26. *Dämmerung* (Zurich, 1934), p. 181; cited in Martin Jay, *The Dialectical Imagination* (Boston, 1973), p. 57.

27. Jay, ibid., p. 57.

28. Cf. especially *Knowledge and Human Interests* and "Technology and Science as Ideology."

29. Cf. *Knowledge and Human Interests* and Introduction to *Theory and Practice*.

30. Cf. *Zur Logik der Sozialwissenschaften* and Appendix to *Knowledge and Human Interests*.

31. Cf. "Technology and Science as Ideology."

32. Introduction to *Theory and Practice*, p. 12.

33. *Theorie der Gesellschaft oder Sozialtechnologie?*, pp. 270ff.

Notes to Preface:

1. The working papers of The Max Planck Institut zur Erforschung der Lebensbedingungen der wissenschaftlich-technischen Welt are referred to in the Notes
as Manuscript MPIL.

2. See also my "Postscript to *Knowledge and Human Interests*," *Philosophy of the
Social Sciences*, 3 (1973): 157–89.

Notes to Part I

Chapter 1

1. C. Offe, "Spätkapitalismus—Versuch einer Begriffsbestimmung," in *Strukturprobleme des kapitalistischen Staates* (Frankfurt, 1972), p. 7ff.

2. K. Löwith, *Meaning in History* (Chicago, 1949).

3. H. P. Dreitzel, ed., *Sozialer Wandel* (Neuwied, 1967); L. Sklair, *The Sociology of
Progress* (London, 1970).

4. R. Koselleck, *Kritik und Krise* (Freiburg, 1961); J. Habermas, *Theory and
Practice* (Boston, 1973), p. 212ff.

5. J. Zelený, *Die Wissenschaftslogik und das Kapital* (Frankfurt, 1968); H.
Reichelt, *Zur logischen Struktur des Kapitalbegriffs bei K. Marx* (Frankfurt,
1970); M. Mauke, *Die Klassentheorie von Marx und Engels* (Frankfurt, 1970);
M. Godelier, "System, Structure and Contradiction in Capital," *The Socialist
Register 1967*, London 1967.

6. M. Jänicke, ed., *Herrschaft und Krise* (Opladen, 1973), especially the contributions of Jänicke, K. W. Deutsch and W. Wagner.

7. [Translator's Note] Following the usage of Niklas Luhmann (currently the most
influential German systems theorist) Habermas typically uses the verb *bestehen*
and its derivatives in phrases referring to problems of structural continuity in
self-regulating systems. Thus, for instance, he speaks of the *Bestandserhaltung
des Systems* (here translated as the "continued existence of the system"),
bestandswichtige Strukturen ("structures important for continued existence"),
and *den Bestand sozialer Systeme* ("the persistence of social systems"). For an
explication of this and other systems-theoretic terminology see the Habermas-
Luhmann debate in *Theorie der Gesellschaft oder Sozialtechnologie?* (Frankfurt,
1971). Luhmann there characterizes the *Bestandsproblem* in terms of the
"permanence," "survival," and "stability" of systems, and distinguishes from it
problems of evolutionary change and advancement (p. 22). Habermas relates
this to a distinction between process—"the performances of a system"—and
structure—"the persistence of a system" (pp. 152–53). In the English literature
on systems theory, problems of continuity and survival are frequently discussed
as problems of "systems maintenance." Because of the variety of syntactical
settings in which Habermas employs *Bestand*, I have found it more convenient
to use "continued existence," "persistence," and, less frequently, "structural

continuity," which also appear in the English literature. For a general discussion of the systems approach see *Modern Systems Research for the Behavioral Scientist*, Walter Buckley, ed. (Chicago, 1968).

8. J. Habermas, N. Luhmann, *Theorie der Gesellschaft oder Sozialtechnologie?* (hereafter *Sozialtechnologie?*) (Frankfurt, 1971), p. 147ff.

9. [Translator's Note] In his discussion of systems theory, Habermas frequently employs the terms *Sollzustand* and *Sollwerte*. Following Parsons—who, with Luhmann, is one of the principle sources and targets of Habermas's discussion— I have rendered the former as "goal state." This refers, of course, to the preferred state that a self-regulating system tends to achieve, and once achieved to maintain, across a wide range of environmental and internal variations. The translation of *Sollwerte* is less obvious as there is, to my knowledge, no standard corresponding English phrase. The state description of a given system involves a specification of the values of the variables characterizing that system. The goal state of a self-regulating system can then be described in terms of those values of the state variables which the system tends to achieve or maintain. (For a general discussion see R. Rudner, *Philosophy of Social Science* (Englewood Cliffs, N.J., 1966), p. 92ff.) In his earlier discussion of Parsons (*Zur Logik der Sozialwissenschaften* (Frankfurt, 1970), p. 164ff.), Habermas introduced the term *Kontrollwerte* in discussing Parsons's version of what is involved in describing the state of a system. Parsons wrote:

> The four exigencies to which a system of action is subject are those of "goal attainment," "adaptation," "integration" and "pattern maintenance." These are dimensions of a space in the sense that a state of the system or of its units' relation to each other may be described, relative to satisfactory points of reference, as "farther along" or less far along on each of these dimensions; a change of state may be described in terms of increases or decreases in the values of each of these variables. ("An Approach to Psychological Theory in Terms of the Theory of Action," in *Psychology: A Study of a Science*, 7 vols. S. Koch, ed. (New York, 1959), 3:631.)

The *Kontrollwerte* then are those values of the variables in the four dimensions that characterize the goal state of the system. To avoid repetition of the cumbersome phrase: "the values of the state variables characteristic of the goal state of a system," I have consistently rendered *Sollwerte* as "goal values." One final complication should be mentioned here. Parsons also uses the term "values" to refer to the cultural values institutionalized in a society. (See, for example, "An Outline of the Social System," in *Theories of Society*, 2 vols. (New York, 1961), 1:30–79). Values in this sense are also relevant to the orientation of a social system for they are "the normative patterns defining, in universalistic terms, the pattern of desirable orientation for the system as a whole" (p. 44). Habermas considers it a fundamental error of Parsons that he supposes the goal values and the cultural values of a social system to be "given." He argues that the goal states of social systems cannot be ascertained in the same way as those of servomechanical or biological systems. Their goal values are not "given";

> they can at best be "found" by way of a political formation of the will. But that would be possible only if one presupposes a general and public discussion by the members of the society based on available information about the given conditions of reproduction of the system. Then a relative agreement could be brought about on a value system that included the objective goal values previously withdrawn from the knowledge and will of the citizens. In such a communication, previously recognized cultural values could not function only as standards; cultural values would themselves be drawn into the discussion, *Zur Logik der Sozialwissenschaften*, pp. 176–77.

10. This concept of anomie was developed in social-scientific literature from Durkheim to Merton and in the investigations of anomic, in particular criminal, behavior which have issued from Merton's work. For a summary, see T. Moser, *Jugendkriminalität und Gesellschaftstruktur* (Frankfurt, 1970).

11. [Translator's Note] The German term is *Steuerungsproblemen*. Where Habermas employs *Steuerung* and compounds thereof, Anglo-American authors use both control and steering, often interchangeably. I have done likewise.

12. P. Berger, T. Luckmann, *The Social Construction of Reality: A Treatise in the Sociology of Knowledge* (Garden City, N.Y., 1966).

13. Phenomenology (A. Schütz) and socio-cybernetics designate conceptual strategies that stylize one or the other of these two aspects. In social-scientific functionalism, attempts have been made to take into account the double aspect of society and to connect the paradigms of life-world and system. (In the *Working Papers* Parsons attempts to connect systems theory and action theory at the categorial level; Etzioni conceives control capacity and consensus formation as two system dimensions; Luhmann gives the phenomenologically introduced, fundamental concept of meaning a systems-theoretic reformulation.) These attempts are instructive for the problem of a suitable conceptualization of social systems, but they do not solve it because the structures of intersubjectivity have not yet been sufficiently examined and the constituents of social systems have not yet been grasped precisely enough.

14. [Translator's Note] The German term is *Kontingenzspielraum*. For an elucidation of this concept see Habermas and Luhmann, *Gesellschaft oder Sozialtechnologie?* According to Luhmann, "the social contingency of meaningful experience is nothing other than an aspect of that boundless world complexity which must be reduced through the formation of systems." From the point of view of systems theory, then, "the social contingency of the world" must be "redefined in terms of complexity" (p. 11). "Complexity," in turn, is a "measure of the number of events and states in the world (world complexity) or of the number of states of a system (intrinsic complexity). With their stabilized

boundaries, systems form and maintain islands of lesser complexity; the order of a system is less probable than that of its environment . . . Its intrinsic complexity must be sufficient to make possible system-maintaining reactions to changes in the environment that affect the system" (pp. 147–48).

15. In what follows, I shall include in "socio-cultural system" the cultural tradition (cultural value systems), as well as the institutions that give these traditions normative power through processes of socialization and professionalization.

16. C. Offe, "Krise und Krisenmanagement," in Jänicke, *Herrschaft und Krise*, p. 197ff.

17. Habermas and Luhmann, *Sozialtechnologie?*, pp. 221ff., 239ff. Luhmann has since developed his theory of communications media as an independent theory *along side of* systems theory and evolution theory.

18. D. Lockwood, "Social Integration and System Integration," in G. Zollschan and W. Hirsch, eds., *Explorations in Social Change* (London, 1964), p. 244ff. This approach has been further developed by Gerhard Brandt.

19. H. M. Baumgartner, *Kontinuität und Geschichte* (Frankfurt, 1972).

20. K. Eder, "Komplexität, Evolution und Geschichte," in F. Maciejewski, ed., Supplement I to *Theorie der Gesellschaft oder Socialtechnologie?* (Frankfurt, 1973), p. 9ff.

Part I, Chapter 2

1. I shall develop this thesis in the framework of a theory of communicative competence.

2. Cf. my "Vorbereitende Bemerkungen zu einer Theorie der kommunikativen Kompetenz," in Habermas and Luhmann, *Sozialtechnologie?*, p. 142ff.

3. I am not claiming that the history of science can be adequately explained by regulators internal to the scientific system. Compare the suggestive theses of G. Böhme, W. van den Daele, and W. Krohn, "Alternativen in der Wissenschaft," *Zeitschrift für Soziologie* (1972): 302ff.; and "Finalisierung der Wissenschaft," ibid. (1973).

4. R. Döbert, G. Nunner, "Konflikt und Rückzugspotentiale in spätkapitalistischen Gesellschaften," *Zeitschrift für Soziologie* (1973), pp. 301–25; R. Döbert, *Die methodologische Bedeutung von Evolutionstheorien für den sozialwissenschaftlichen Funktionalismus—diskutiert am Beispiel der Evolution von Religionssystemen* (diss., Phil., University of Frankfurt, 1973); cf. also the interesting construction of N. Luhmann, *Religion—System und Sozialisation* (Neuwied, 1973), p. 15ff.

5. On the concept of developmental logic in cognitive developmental psychology see L. Kohlberg, "Stage and Sequence: The Cognitive Developmental Approach to Socialization," in D. A. Goslin, ed., *Handbook of Socialization* (Chicago, 1969), p. 347ff.

6. K. Eder, *Mechanismen der sozialen Evolution* (Manuscript, MPIL).

7. A. Mitscherlich, *Krankheit als Konflikt*, 2 vols. (Frankfurt, 1966/67); K. Brede, *Sozioanalyse psychosomatischer Störungen* (Frankfurt, 1972).

8. H. Plessner, *Die Stufen des Organischen und der Mensch* (Berlin, 1928).

9. Habermas and Luhmann, *Sozialtechnologie?*, p. 155ff.

10. Thus, in the systems theories of social development of K. W. Deutsch (*The Nerves of Government* [New York, 1963]) and A. Eztzioni (*The Active Society* [New York, 1968]), concepts of learning rightly play a central role in the analysis; of course, these concepts are too narrow to encompass discursive learning.

11. J. Habermas, "Wahrheitstheorien," in *Wirklichkeit und Reflexion: Festschrift für Walter Schulz* (Pfullingen, 1973), pp. 211–65. On the logic of discourse, see S. Toulmin, *The Uses of Argument* (Cambridge, 1964); and P. Edwards, *Logic of Moral Discourse* (New York, 1955).

12. J. Habermas, "Wozu noch Philosophie?" in *Philosophisch-politische Profile* (Frankfurt, 1971), English translation, *Social Research*, vol. 40, 1974.

13. On this concept compare N. Luhmann, "Wirtschaft als soziales Problem," in *Soziologische Aufklärung* (Opladen, 1970), p. 226ff.

Part I, Chapter 3.

1. [Translator's Note] Habermas uses the term *vorhochkulturell* to designate social formations that do not generally meet the criteria of civilizations (*Hochkulturen*). (For a brief characterization of these criteria see *Toward a Rational Society*, Boston, 1970, p. 94ff.) Included in the class of "pre-civilizations" are the more primitive societies characteristic of the "long initial phase until the end of the Mesolithic period," as well as the "first settled cultures based on the domestication of animals and the cultivation of plants" (*Toward a Rational Society*, p. 114). There is, to my knowledge, no exactly corresponding term in English anthropological literature. "Pre-civilization" seems unnecessarily cumbersome. The characteristics of such societies stressed by Habermas in what follows are those generally associated with "primitive" societies. I have therefore, with Habermas' agreement, employed this more usual terminology.

2. D. Bell, "The Post-Industrial Society: The Evolution of an Idea," in *Survey* (1971): 102ff.

3. T. Parsons, *Societies: Evolutionary and Comparative Perspectives* (Englewood Cliffs, 1966); G. Lenski, *Power and Privilege* (New York, 1966); Sahlins, *Service, Evolution and Culture* (Ann Arbor, 1968); further literature in Eder, *Mechanismen der sozialen Evolution*.

4. [Translator's Note] For an elucidation of the concept of instrumental action see Habermas, *Toward a Rational Society*, pp. 91–94 and *Knowledge and Human Interests* (Boston, 1971).

5. C. Levi-Strauss, *The Savage Mind* (Chicago, 1966).

6. R. L. Caneiro, "A Theory of the Origin of the State," *Science* (1970): 733ff.

7. Ibid., pp. 736ff.

8. [Translator's Note] *Herrschaft*, literally "lordship," can be employed with various nuances in German social thought and has, for this reason, no adequate English equivalent. Parsons translates the term as "imperative co-ordination"

and "authority" in his edition of Weber's *Theory of Social and Economic Organization* (New York, 1947), p. 152ff., 342ff. This translation reflects Parson's interpretation of Weber's position on value-neutrality in social science. Whatever the merits of his case (see G. Roth and C. Wittich, eds., *Economy and Society*, 3 vols., New York, 1968, for a critique of his translation), Habermas certainly wishes to retain the valuational nuances associated with the term. Thus, "domination" seems the more appropriate translation in many contexts. I have used both "authority" and "domination," and less frequently "rule," according to the context.

9. I am using the expression "private" here, not in the sense of modern bourgeois civil law [*Privatrechts*], but in the sense of a "privileged" disposition.

10. [Translator's Note] Unfortunately, there is no English equivalent for the important term *Naturwüchsigkeit*. The suffix -*wüchsig* (from *wachsen*, to grow) means literally "growing." *Naturwüchsig* is used by critical theorists to refer to structures that develop spontaneously, without reflection or plan. It is employed by way of contrast to consciously directed processes, to structures that are the result of human will and determination. I have translated *Naturwüchsigkeit* here—somewhat awkwardly—as "unplanned, nature-like development."

11. Compare the historical studies of the concept by M. Riedel, *Studien zu Hegels Rechtsphilosophie* (Frankfurt, 1969); see also his *Bürgerliche Gesellschaft und Staat bei Hegel* (Neuwied, 1970).

12. Max Weber, *Wirtschaft und Gesellschaft* (Köln, 1956), p. 1034ff.; English translation edited by G. Roth, C. Wittich, *Economy and Society*, 3 vols., (New York, 1968).

13. Cf. also N. Luhmann, "Knappheit, Geld und die bürgerliche Gesellschaft," in *Jahrbuch für Sozialwissenschaft*, Bd. 23 (1972), p. 186ff.

14. This is a model that is intended to characterize the zenith of a very complex historical process of development. On the systematic history of capitalism, the best total presentation is still that of M. Dobb, *Studies in the Development of Capitalism* (London, 1947).

15. On the concepts "interest-guided" versus "value-oriented" cf. Habermas and Luhmann, *Sozialtechnologie?*, p. 251ff.

16. O. Brunner, "Das Zeitalter der Ideologien," in *Neue Wege zur Sozialgeschichte* (Göttingen, 1956); K. Lenk, ed., *Ideologie* (Neuwied, 1961).

Part I, Chapter 4

1. Cf. my "Vorbereitende Bemerkungen zu einer Theorie der kommunikativen Kompetenz."

2. H. Pilot attempts a similar reconstruction of "dialectic" in "Jürgen Habermas's Empirically Falsified Philosophy of History," in *The Positivist Dispute in German Sociology* (London/New York, 1975).

3. J. Habermas, *Knowledge and Human Interests* (Boston, 1971), esp. p. 187ff.

4. H. Neuendorff, *Der Begriff des Interesses* (Frankfurt, 1973).

5. Today Adorno's works are exemplary for a critique of culture that constantly

refers back to a critique of commodity fetishism; see T. W. Adorno, "Kulturkritik und Gesellschaft," in *Prismen* (Frankfurt, 1955), p. 7ff.; English trans., *Prisms* (London, 1967).

6. S. Tsuru, *Has Capitalism Changed?* (Tokyo, 1961).

Notes to Part II

Chapter 1

1. See, for example, B. E. Hobsbawm, *Age of Revolution: Seventeen Eighty-Nine to Eighteen Forty-Eight* (New York, 1962).

2. St. Hymer, "Multinationale Konzerne und das Gesetz der ungleichen Entwicklung" and J. O'Connor, "Die Bedeutung des ökonomischen Imperialismus," both in D. Senghaas, ed., *Imperialismus und strukturelle Gewalt* (Frankfurt, 1972).

3. M. D. Reagan, *The Managed Economy* (New York, 1963); A. Shonfield, *Modern Capitalism* (London, 1965); P. K. Crosser, *State Capitalism in the Economy of the U.S.* (New York, 1960); J. Galbraith, *The New Industrial State* (Boston, 1967); M. Weidenbaum, *The Modern Public Sector* (New York, 1969); and S. Melman, *Pentagon Capitalism* (New York, 1970).

4. J. O'Connor, *The Fiscal Crisis of the State* (New York, 1973). O'Connor's three-sector model is developed with America in mind; presumably, it would have to be modified for the Federal Republic and other European countries. Cf. the reflections on this in U. Rödel, *Zusammenfassung kritischer Argumente zum Status der Werttheorie und zur Möglichkeit einer werttheoretischen Krisentheorie* (Manuscript, MPIL).

5. [Translator's Note] *Bildung*, generally "formation," can also be used more narrowly to connote processes of overall spiritual development or their completion, that is, "education," "cultivation." Jeremy Shapiro renders *Willensbildung*—literally "will-formation"—as "decision-making," while noting that it "emphasizes the process (of deliberation and discourse) through which a decision was 'formed,' not the moment at which it was 'made.' " (*Toward a Rational Society*, Boston, 1971, "Translator's Preface," p. vii.) Since one of the principal concerns of the present work is the elucidation and defense of a model of discursive formation of will, I have found it advisable to use the more literal renditions "will-formation" and "formation of the will."

6. On the functionalist concept of the procurement of legitimation, see T. Parsons, "Voting and Equilibrium of the American Political System," in E. Burdick and A. Brodbeck, *American Voting Behavior* (Glencoe, Ill., 1959).

7. Compare my introduction to J. Habermas, L. v. Friedeburg, Ch. Oehler, F. Weltz, *Student und Politik* (Neuwied, 1961); and J. Habermas, *Strukturwandel der Öffentlichkeit* (Neuwied, 1962).

8. J. Habermas, *Toward a Rational Society* (Boston, 1971), p. 102ff.

9. J. Schumpeter, *Capitalism, Socialism and Democracy*, 3rd. ed., (New York, 1950).

10. For example, Rathenau, Berle and Means.

11. C. Offe, "Politische Herrschaft und Klassenstrukturen," in Kress and Senghass, eds., *Politikwissenschaft* (Frankfurt, 1969), p. 155ff.; English translation, "Political Authority and Class Structure—An Analysis of Late Capitalist Societies," in *International Journal of Sociology* (Spring, 1972), pp. 73–108.

12. J. Strachey, *Contemporary Capitalism* (New York, 1956).

13. J. O'Connor, *The Fiscal Crisis of the State.*

14. W. Vogt, "Eine Theorie der ökonomischen Stagnation," in *Leviathan*, H. 2 (1973).

15. C. Offe, "Politische Herrschaft und Klassenstrukturen."

16. N. Luhmann, "Knappheit, Geld und bürgerliche Gesellschaft," *op. cit.*

17. U. Rödel, *Zusammenfassung kritischer Argumente.*

Part II, Chapter 2

1. J. Galtung, "Eine strukturelle Theorie des Imperialismus" in D. Senghaas, ed., *Imperialismus und strukturelle Gewalt* (Frankfurt, 1972); also F. Fröbel, J. Heinrichs, O. Kreye, O. Sunkel, "Kapital und Arbeitskraft," in *Leviathan*, 4 (1973) p. 429ff.

2. D. L. Meadows, D. H. Meadows, *Limits to Growth* (New York, 1972).

3. K. M. Meyer-Abich, "Die ökologische Grenze des Wirtschaftswachstums," in *Umschau* 72 (1972), H. 20, p. 645ff.

4. Cf. below, Part III, Chapter 5.

5. N. Luhmann, "Soziologie des politischen Systems," in *Soziologische Aufklärung* (Opladen, 1970), p. 170.

6. C. F. v. Weizsäcker, ed., *Kriegsfolgen und Kriegsverhütung* (München, 1971), introduction.

Part II, Chapter 3

1. Cf. E. Mandel, *Der Spätkapitalismus* (Frankfurt, 1972).

2. J. Hirsch, *Wissenschaftlich-technischer Fortschritt und politisches System* (Frankfurt, 1970), p. 248ff.

3. C. Offe, "Tauschverhältnis und politische Steuerung," in *Strukturprobleme des kapitalistischen Staates* (Frankfurt, 1972), p. 27ff.

4. H. Marcuse develops this thesis in *Counterrevolution and Revolt* (Boston, 1972).

5. R. Döbert, *Die methodologische Bedeutung von Evolutionstheorien, loc. cit.*

Part II, Chapter 4

1. Marx developed this conception in *The Eighteenth Brumaire of Louis Bonaparte* (New York, 1963). Cf. also N. Poulantzas, "The Problem of the Capitalist State," in *New Left Review* (1969), p. 67ff.

2. W. Müller, Ch. Neusüss, "Die Sozialstaatsillusion," in *SoPo* (1970), p. 4ff.; E.

Altvater, "Zu einigen Problemen des Staatsinterventionismus," in Jänicke, ed., *Herrschaft und Krise*, p. 170ff.

3. Altvater, *op. cit.*, p. 181.

4. Müller, Neusüss, *op. cit.*

5. O'Connor, *The Fiscal Crisis of the State*.

6. The analytical distinctions proposed here have arisen out of discussions with Sigrid Meuschel.

7. P. Mattick, *Marx and Keynes* (Boston, 1969), p. 128ff, 188ff.; U. Rödel, *Forschungsprioritäten und technologische Entwicklung* (Frankfurt, 1972), p. 32ff.

8. On this point, most recently, H. Holländer, *Das Gesetz des tendenziellen Falls der Profitrate* (Regensburg, 1972), Diskussionsbeiträge zur Wirtschaftswissenschaft.

9. E. Altvater, F. Huiskens, eds., *Materialien zur Politischen Ökonomie des Ausbildungssektors* (Erlangen, 1971).

10. A. Sohn-Rethel, *Die ökonomische Doppelnatur des Spätkapitalismus* (Neuwied, 1972), traces the altered production of surplus value to changes in the structure of production and wages.

11. O'Connor distinguishes absolute, relative, and "indirect" production of surplus value.

12. *Capital*, 3 vols. (International Publishers: New York, 1967), 1:609.

13. U. Rödel, *Zusammenfassung kritischer Argumente*.

14. R. Hilferding introduced this expression.

15. Marx speaks of the historical and moral element in the determination of the value of the commodity "labor power"; *Capital*, 1:165.

16. Institut für Gesellschaftswissenschaften of the Zentralkomitee of the Sozialistische Einheitspartei Deutschlands, ed., *Imperialismus heute* (Berlin, 1965); R. Gündel, H. Heininger, P. Hess, K. Zieschang, *Zur Theorie des staatsmonopolistischen Kapitalismus* (Berlin, 1967).

17. M. Wirth, *Kapitalismustheorie in der DDR* (Frankfurt, 1972).

18. J. Hirsch, "Funktionsveränderungen der Staatsverwaltung in spätkapitalistischen Industriegesellschaften," in *Blätter für deutsche und internationale Politik* (1969), p. 150ff.

19. C. Offe. "Klassenherrschaft und politisches System. Die Selektivität politischer Institutionen," in *Strukturprobleme des kapitalistischen Staates* (Frankfurt, 1972), p. 66ff.

20. Ibid., p. 78ff.

Part II, Chapter 5

1. J. Hirsch, *Wissenschaftlich-technischer Fortschritt*, p. 248ff.

2. C. Offe speaks of a "political dilemma of technocracy."

3. This is a consequence of the penetration of systems-theoretic *language* into the self-understanding of the state administration.

4. St. Cohen, *Modern Capitalist Planning* (Cambridge, 1969).

5. H. Arndt, *Die Konzentration der westdeutschen Wirtschaft* (Pfullingen, 1966); J. Hufschmid, *Die Politik des Kapitals* (Frankfurt, 1970); G. Kolko, *Wealth and Power in America: An Analysis of Social Class and Income Distribution* (New York, 1962).

6. F. W. Scharpf, "Planung als politischer Prozess," in *Die Verwaltung* (1971); and "Komplexität als Schranke der politischen Planung," in *Politische Vierteljahreschrift*, Sonderheft *4* (1972):168ff.

7. R. Funke, *Exkurs über Planungsrationalität* (Manuscript, MPIL) and *Organisationsstrukturen planender Verwaltung* (Diss., University of Darmstadt, 1973).

8. C. Offe, "Tauschverhältnis und politische Steuerung," p. 27ff.

9. F. Naschold, *Organisation und Demokratie* (Stuttgart, 1969); "Komplexität und Demokratie," in *Politische Vierteljahreschrift* (1968), p. 494ff; see Luhmann's critique and Naschold's reply in *Politische Vierteljahreschrift* (1969), pp. 324ff., 326ff.; see also S. and W. Streeck, *Parteiensystem und Status quo* (Frankfurt, 1972).

Part II, Chapter 6

1. M. Edelmann, *The Symbolic Uses of Politics* (Chicago, 1964) and *Politics as Symbolic Action* (Chicago, 1971).

2. H. G. Gadamer, *Wahrheit und Methode* (Tübingen, 1969).

3. A. Wellmer, *Critical Theory of Society* (New York, 1971), p. 41ff.

4. J. Habermas, "Bewusstmachende oder rettende Kritik?," in *Zur Aktualität Walter Benjamins* (Frankfurt, 1972), p. 173ff.

5. In the Federal Republic the discussion was touched off by S. B. Robinsohn, *Bildungsreform als Revision des Curriculum* (Neuwied, 1967).

6. U. Oevermann develops interesting arguments in a manuscript on the research strategy of the Institut für Bildungsforschung (Berlin, 1970).

7. H. E. Bahr, ed., *Politisierung des Alltags* (Neuwied, 1972); Offe, "Bürgerinitiativen," in *Strukturprobleme*, p. 153ff.

8. R. Mayntz, "Funktionen der Beteiligung bei öffentlicher Planung," in *Demokratie und Verwaltung* (Berlin, 1972), p. 341ff.

9. On this point see H. P. Widmaier, *Machtstrukturen im Wohlfahrtsstaat*, Regensburger Diskussionsbeiträge zur Wirtschaftswissenschaft (1973).

10. Shonfield, *Modern Capitalism*.

11. Offe, "Krisen und Krisenmanagement," p. 220.

Part II, Chapter 7

1. J. Habermas, *Zur Logik der Sozialwissenschaften*, p. 290ff.

2. The failure of the "basic personality approach" in cultural anthropology shows that simple transmission assumptions are incorrect. A plausible model of socialization is contained in the project proposal of Oevermann, Kräppner, and Krappmann, "Elternhaus und Schule" (Manuscript, Institut für Bildungsforschung, Berlin).

3. A correspondence between normative and motivational structures is most likely

for the ontogenetic levels of moral consciousness. Cf. L. Kohlberg, "Stage and Sequence: The Cognitive Developmental Approach to Socialization," in D. Goslin, ed., *Handbook of Socialization Theory and Research* (Chicago, 1969), p. 397ff.

4. Habermas, "Natural Law and Revolution," in *Theory and Practice* (Boston, 1973), p. 82ff.

5. G. A. Almond and S. Verba, *The Civic Culture* (Boston, 1965).

6. On the historical background of this category see C. B. Macpherson, *The Political Theory of Possessive Individualism: Hobbes to Locke* (London and New York, 1962).

7. M. Müller, H. Bredekamp, et al., *Autonomie der Kunst* (Frankfurt, 1972).

8. H. Marcuse, *Counterrevolution and Revolt* (Boston, 1972).

9. D. Käsler, ed., *Max Weber* (München, 1972); W. Schluchter, *Aspekte bürokratischer Herrschaft* (München, 1972), p. 236ff.

10. R. Döbert, G. Nunner, *Konflikt- und Rückzugspotentiale*.

11. G. Nunner-Winkler, *Chancengleichheit und individuelle Förderung* (Stuttgart, 1971).

12. D. Hartung, R. Nuthmann, W. C. Winterhager, *Politologen im Beruf* (Stuttgart, 1970); W. Armbruster, H. J. Bodenhöfer, H. J. Hartung, R. Nuthmann, "*Expansion und Innovation*," Manuscript, Institut für Bildungsforschung (Berlin, 1972).

13. C. Offe, *Leistungsprinzip und industrielle Arbeit* (Frankfurt, 1970).

14. See Part II, Chapter 5.

15. R. Bendix, *Der Glaube an die Wissenschaft* (Konstanz, 1971).

16. J. Mittelstrass, *Das praktische Fundament der Wissenschaft* (Konstanz, 1972).

17. A. Hauser, *The Social History of Art*, 4 vols. (New York, 1957).

18. D. Bell, "The Cultural Contradictions of Capitalism," *Public Interest* (Fall 1970):16ff.

19. K. Keniston, *Youth and Dissent* (New York, 1971), p. 387ff.

20. R. Döbert, G. Nunner, *Konflikt- und Rückzugspotentiale loc. cit.*

21. K. Keniston, *Young Radicals* (New York, 1968).

22. R. Döbert, G. Nunner, *Konflikt- und Rückzugspotentiale*; O. Negt and A. Kluge attempt a theoretically ambitious interpretation of the *experiential* content of the student revolts in *Öffentlichkeit und Erfahrung. Zur Organisationsanalyse von bürgerlicher und proletarischer Öffentlichkeit* (Frankfurt, 1972).

Notes to Part III

Chapter 1

1. M. Weber, "The Types of Legitimate Domination," in *Economy and Society*, G. Roth, C. Wittich, eds., 3 vols. (New York, 1968), 1:212ff.

2. M. Weber, ibid., 3:953.

3. G. Lenski, *Power and Privilege* p. 43ff.

4. M. Weber, *Economy and Society*, 1:214.

5. Ibid., p. 213.

6. Ibid., 3:953.

7. Ibid., 1:217ff., 3:956ff.

8. Ch. Siara, *Bürgerliches Formalrecht bei Max Weber*, Diplomarbeit (Frankfurt, 1968).

9. Luhmann, "Soziologie des politischen Systems," p. 167.

10. N. Luhmann, "Positives Recht und Ideologie," in *Soziologische Aufklärung* (Opladen, 1970), p. 180.

11. N. Luhmann, *Legitimation durch Verfahren* (Neuwied, 1969), p. 51.

12. Ibid., p. 139.

13. Ibid., p. 240.

14. "Structures reduce the extreme complexity of the world to a much narrowed and simplified domain of expectations which are presupposed as premises of behavior and normally not themselves questioned. They are always based, therefore, on *deceptions* . . . especially about the actual action-potential of men, and for this reason they must be arranged so as to take account of disappointments." Ibid., p. 233ff.

15. [Translator's Note] For Weber's distinction between *zweckrational* ("purposive-rational," that is, means-ends oriented) and *wertrational* ("rationally oriented to value," that is, to the realization of certain values) see his discussion of "The Types of Social Action," in *Economy and Society*, vol. 1.

16. J. Winckelmann, *Legitimität und Legalität in Max Webers Herrschaftssoziologie* (Tübingen, 1952), p. 75ff.

17. Ibid., p. 72ff.

18. K. Jaspers, *Max Weber* (Oldenburg, 1932); English trans. in *Three Essays: Leonardo, Descartes, Max Weber* (New York, 1964). Compare W. J. Mommsen, *Max Weber und die deutsche Politik* (Tübingen, 1959), p. 418. "If Winckelmann wants to show that there are in Weber's theory of democratic authority so-called 'immanent limits to legitimation' of a value-oriented nature, then this is simply a misinterpretation."

19. Habermas and Luhmann, *Sozialtechnologie?*, p. 243ff.

Part III, Chapter 2

1. K. R. Popper, *The Open Society and Its Enemies*, 2 vols. (Princeton, 1950), vol. 1, chap. 5, "Nature and Convention."

2. L. Stevenson, *Ethics and Language* (New Haven, 1950); D. H. Monro, *Empiricism and Ethics* (Cambridge, 1967).

3. R. M. Hare, *The Language of Morals* (Oxford, 1952).

4. K. H. Ilting, "Anerkennung," in *Probleme der Ethik* (Freiburg, 1972).

5. H. Albert, *Traktat über kritische Vernunft* (Tübingen, 1968), chap. 3, p. 55ff. J. Mittelstrass (*Das praktische Fundament der Wissenschaft*, p. 18) is certainly correct in remarking that the trilemma of Popper and Albert results from the ungrounded equation of deductive justification [*Begründung*] with justification in general. K. O. Apel, *Das Apriori der Kommunikationsgemeinschaft*, vol. II of

Transformation der Philosophie (Frankfurt, 1973), p. 405ff., distinguishes deductive from transcendental justification and traces the unreflectiveness of critical rationalism to a characteristic neglect of the pragmatic dimension of argumentation.

Under the presupposition of abstracting from the pragmatic dimension of signs there is no human *subject* of argumentation and therefore also no possibility of a reflection on the conditions of possibility of argumentation which are *always presupposed by us*. Instead, there is the infinite hierarchy of *meta*-languages, *meta*-theories, etc., in which the *reflective competence* of man as the *subject of argumentation* is simultaneously made perceptible and concealed . . . And yet we know very well that our *reflective competence*—more precisely, the self-reflection of the human subject of thought operations, which is bracketed out *a priori* at the level of syntactic-semantic systems—is hidden behind the aporia of infinite regress and makes possible, for example, something like an undecidability *proof* in the sense of Gödel. In other words, precisely in the confirmation that the subjective conditions of possibility of argumentation *cannot be objectivated* in a syntactic-semantic *model* of argumentation is expressed the self-reflective knowledge of the transcendental-pragmatic subject of argumentation (p. 406ff).

6. Albert, *Trakatat über kritische Vernunft*, p. 78.
7. J. Dewey, *The Quest for Certainty* (New York, 1929).
8. S. Toulmin, *The Uses of Argument;* on Peirce see K. O. Apel, "Von Kant zu Peirce. Die semiotische Transformation der Transzendentalen Logik," in *Transformation der Philosophie*, 2:157ff.
9. J. Habermas, "Wahrheitstheorien."
10. R. Grice, *The Grounds of Moral Judgement* (Cambridge, 1967).
11. K. Baier, *The Moral Point of View* (Ithaca, 1958); M. G. Singer, *Generalization in Ethics* (London, 1963).
12. P. Lorenzen, *Normative Logic and Ethics* (Mannheim, 1969); "Szientismus versus Dialektik," in *Festschrift für Gadamer* (Tübingen, 1970), 1:57ff.; O. Schwemmer, *Philosophie der Praxis* (Frankfurt, 1971); S. Blasche and O. Schwemmer, "Methode und Dialektik," in M. Riedel, ed., *Rehabilitierung der praktischen Philosophie I*, (Freiburg, 1972), p. 457ff.
13. P. Lorenzen, *Normative Logic and Ethics*, p. 74.
14. O. Schwemmer, *Philosophie der Praxis*, p. 194.
15. Cited from manuscript; soon to appear in a volume on practical philosophy edited by F. Kambartel for the *Theorie-Diskussion* series, Suhrkamp Verlag.
16. Cf. also K. O. Apel, "Das Apriori der Kommunikationsgemeinschaft und die Ethik," in *Transformation der Philosophie*, 2:358ff. In this fascinating essay, in which Apel summarizes his large-scale attempt at reconstruction, the fundamental assumption of communicative ethics is developed: "with the presupposition of intersubjective consensus the search for truth must also anticipate the

morality of an ideal communication community." (p. 405) Even with Apel there arises, to be sure, a residual decisionistic problematic.

> Whoever poses the—in my opinion, quite meaningful—question of the justification of the moral principle already *takes part* in the discussion. And one can "make him aware"—quite in the manner proposed by Lorenzen and Schwemmer of a reconstruction of reason—of what he has "already" accepted, and that he should accept this principle through intentional affirmation as the *condition of the possibility and of the validity of argumentation.* Whoever does not comprehend or accept this withdraws from the discussion. But anyone who does not participate in the discussion cannot pose the question of the justification of fundamental ethical principles. Thus, it is *meaningless* to talk of the meaninglessness of his question and to recommend to him a valiant decision to believe." (pp. 420–21)

That "intentional affirmation" can, however, only be stylized to an intentional act as long as one disregards the fact that discourses are not only contingently, but systematically admitted into a life-context whose peculiarly fragile *facticity consists* in the recognition of discursive-validity claims. Anyone who does not participate, or is not ready to participate in argumentation stands nevertheless "already" in contexts of *communicative action.* In doing so, he has already naively recognized the validity claims—however counterfactually raised—that are contained in speech acts and that can be redeemed only discursively. Otherwise he would have had to detach himself from the communicatively established language game of everyday practice. The *fundamental* error of methodological solipsism extends to the assumption of the possibility not only of monological *thought,* but also of monological *action.* It is absurd to imagine that a subject capable of speech and action could permanently realize the limit case of communicative action, that is, the monological role of acting instrumentally and strategically, without losing his identity. The socio-cultural form of life of communicatively socialized individuals produces the "transcendental illusion" of pure communicative action in *every* interaction context and, at the same time, it structurally refers *every* interaction context to the possibility of an ideal speech situation in which the validity claims accepted in action can be tested discursively. (Habermas and Luhmann, *Sozialtechnologie?*, p. 136ff.) If one understands the communication community *in the first place* as a community of interaction and not of argumentation, as action and not as discourse, then the relation—important from the perspective of emancipation—of the "real" to the "ideal" communication community (Apel, "Das Apriori der Kommunikationsgemeinschaft," p. 429ff.) can also be examined from the point of view of idealizations of pure communicative action (cf. my introduction to the English edition of *Theory and Practice,* Boston, 1973, p. 1ff., and my "Postscript to *Knowledge and Human Interests," Philosophy of the Social Sciences, 3* (1973): p. 157–89).

Part III, Chapter 3

1. H. Schelsky, "Mehr Demokratie oder mehr Freiheit?," *Frankfurter Allgemeine Zeitung*, Jan. 20, 1973, p. 7.
2. J. Habermas, "Der Universalitätsanspruch der Hermeneutik," in *Hermeneutik und Ideologiekritik* (Frankfurt, 1971), p. 120ff.
3. P. Lorenzen, "Szientismus versus Dialektik."
4. J. Habermas, "Einige Bemerkungen zum Problem der Begründung von Werturteilen," in *Verhandlungen des 9. Deutschen Kongress für Philosophie* (Meisenheim, 1972), p. 89ff.
5. C. Offe, "Klassenherrschaft und politisches System," p. 85.
6. Habermas, *Knowledge and Human Interests*, p. 284ff.
7. Compare the abovementioned dissertation of R. Döbert; also G. Schmid, "N. Luhmanns funktional-strukturelle Systemtheorie," in *Politische Vierteljahreschrift* (1970), p. 186ff.
8. J. Habermas, *Toward a Rational Society*, p. 74ff.

Part III, Chapter 4

1. P. Berger, *The Sacred Canopy* (New York, 1967), p. 22ff.
2. On this point compare the anthropological investigations of Lévi-Strauss, *Totemism* (London, 1964), *Structural Anthropology* (New York, 1963), *The Raw and the Cooked: An Introduction to a Science of Mythology I* (New York, 1970), and *From Honey to Ashes: An Introduction to a Science of Mythology II* (New York, 1973).
3. Cf. T. Rendtorff, *Theorie des Christentums* (Gütersloh, 1972), p. 96ff.
4. C. F. von Weizsäcker, *Die Einheit der Natur* (Stuttgart, 1971).
5. F. Nietzsche, *The Will to Power* (New York, 1967), Preface, p. 4.
6. F. Nietzsche, *Werke*, K. Schlechta, ed., Bd. III, p. 480.
7. Habermas, "Natural Law and Revolution," in *Theory and Practice*, p. 82ff.
8. P. Bachrach, *Die Theorie der demokratischen Eliteherrschaft* (Frankfurt, 1967).
9. Ibid., p. 8.
10. M. Landmann, *Das Ende des Individuums* (Stuttgart, 1971).
11. A. Wellmer, *Critical Theory of Society*, pp. 130–31. (I have retranslated the lines quoted in the text. T. McC.)
12. H. Schelsky, "Der Mensch in der wissenschaftlichen Zivilisation," in *Auf der Suche nach Wirchlichkeit* (Düsseldorf, 1965), p. 468.
13. H. Schelsky, *Ortsbestimmung der deutschen Soziologie* (Düsseldorf, 1959), p. 96ff.
14. H. Schelsky, "Der Mensch in der wissenschaftlichen Zivilisation," p. 471.
15. H. Schelsky, "Ist Dauerreflexion institutionalisierbar?," in *Auf der Suche nach Wirchlichkeit*, p. 250ff.
16. T. W. Adorno, *Minima Moralia* (Frankfurt, 1951), p. 251ff. (English translation, E. Jephcott, *Minima Moralia* [London, 1974]).
17. B. Willms, "Revolution oder Protest," p. 11, and "System und Subjekt," in *Theorie der Gesellschaft oder Sozialtechnologie?*, Supplement I.
18. T. W. Adorno, *Minima Moralia*, p. 109.

19. L. S. Feuer, "What is Alienation? The Career of a Concept," in M. Stein, A. Vidich, eds., *Sociology on Trial* (Englewood Cliffs, N.J., 1963); cf. also the work of K. Kenniston, R. D. Laing, G. Sykes, and the literature on anomie, "urban problems," identity problems, etc.
20. A. Etzioni, *The Active Society* (New York, 1968), p. 618.
21. Ibid., p. 619.
22. Ibid., p. 633ff.

Part III, Chapter 5

1. Habermas and Luhmann, *Sozialtechnologie?*, p. 293.
2. Ibid., p. 326ff.
3. Ibid., p. 327.
4. Ibid.
5. W. D. Narr, C. Offe, *Wohlfahrtsstaat und Massenloyalität* (Köln, 1973), Introduction.
6. Habermas and Luhmann, *Sozialtechnologie?*, p. 300ff.
7. Luhmann, "Komplexitat und Demokratie," p. 316.
8. Ibid., p. 317.
9. N. Luhmann, "Politikbegriffe und die 'Politisierung' der Verwaltung," in *Demokratie und Verwaltung* (Berlin, 1972), p. 221.
10. Ibid., p. 220.
11. Luhmann, "Komplexitat und Demokratie," p. 319.
12. N. Luhmann, *Politische Planung* (Opladen, 1971), Preface.
13. L. C. Gawthrop, *Administrative Politics and Social Change* (New York 1971); Ronge and Schmieg, eds., *Politische Planung in Theorie und Praxis* (München, 1972), Introduction; cf. also his *Restriktionen politischer Planung* (Dissertation, Bremen, 1972), esp. chaps. 1 and 5.
14. Luhmann, "Politikbegriffe und die 'Politisierung' der Verwaltung," p. 225.
15. Gawthrop, *Administrative Politics*, p. 42ff.
16. Luhmann, "Politikbegriffe," p. 225; "Selbstthematisierungen des Gesellschaftssystems," *Zeitschrift für Soziologie* (1973), p. 21ff.
17. F. Naschold, "Zur Politik und Ökonomie der Planung," in *Politische Vierteljahreschrift*, Sonderheft 4 (1972), p. 13ff.
18. N. Luhmann, "Politikbegriffe," p. 224.
19. Ibid., p. 227ff.
20. A. Gehlen, "Über Kristallisation," in *Studien zur Anthropologie* (Neuwied, 1963), p. 311ff.
21. F. Naschold, "Politik und Ökonomie," p. 43.
22. Ibid., p. 43.
23. Scharpf, "Komplexität als Schranke der politischen Planung," p. 169.
24. Ibid., p. 177.
25. M. Fester, "Vorstudien zu einer Theorie kommunikativer Planung," *ARCH* (1970), p. 43ff.
26. R. Mayntz, ed., *Bürokratische Organisation* (Köln, 1968), and *Formalisierte Modelle in der Soziologie* (Neuwied, 1967).

27. Etzioni, *The Active Society*, p. 622ff.
28. See above, Part I.
29. M. Fester, "Vorstudien zu einer Theorie kommunikativer Planung," p. 67ff.; cf. also the results of an investigation by the Battelle-Institut: BMBW, *Methoden der Prioritätenbestimmung I* (Bonn, 1971).

Part III, Chapter 6

1. Offe has developed experimental reflections on a theory of actionism.

> The problem for a theory of the state that wants to prove the class character of political domination consists thus in the fact that it cannot at all be carried through *as a theory*, as an objectivating presentation of state functions and their relation to interests. Only the practice of class struggle redeems its cognitive claim . . . this limitation of the theoretical cognitive power is not conditioned by the inadequacy of its methods but by the structure of its object. The latter *evades* its class-theoretic elucidation. Simplifying, one can say that political domination in capitalist industrial societies is the method of class domination which *does not reveal itself* as such. Offe, *Strukturprobleme*, pp. 90–91.

Offe starts from the thesis that the class character of the state, which he asserts, is not at all accessible to objectivating knowledge. In my opinion, we do not need to share this premise, since the model—introduced above—of suppressed but generalizable interests can indeed be applied to a reconstruction of non-decisions, selection rules, and latency phenomena. Even if we had to share Offe's premises, his argumentation would remain inconsistent. Let us assume that the goal of removing a class structure could be grounded from the following point of view:

—a practice that can justify itself is an independent, that is, rational practice;
—the demand for a justifiable practice is rational wherever political consequences can result from actions;
—hence, it is rational to desire the transformation of a social system that can advance normative-validity claims only counterfactually, that is, that cannot justify its practice because it structurally suppresses generalizable interests.

If the class character of our system of domination were, as Offe states, not recognizable, revolutionary action would be able to base itself at best on conjectures that turn out, retrospectively, to be true or false. As long as class character is not recognized, political action cannot be justified on the basis of generalizable interests; it remains an irrational practice. An irrational practice (whatever goals it may claim for itself) cannot be singled out from any *other* given practice (even from an avowedly fascist one) *with grounds*. Indeed, in so far as such a practice is carried through with will and consciousness, it contradicts *the* (and precisely the) only justifications that can be laid claim to for the transformation of a class structure.

Such considerations need hinder no one from accepting a decisionistic action pattern—often enough there is no alternative. But in that case one acts subjectively and, in weighing the risks, *can* know that the political consequences of this action are only calculable in moral terms. Even then one must still presuppose a trust in the power of practical reason. Indeed, even one who doubts practical reason *itself* could know that he is not only acting subjectively but is also placing his action outside of the domain of argumentation in general. But then a *theory* of actionism is also superfluous. The execution of an action has to be sufficient unto itself. *Unjustifiable* hopes that are tied to the success of an action can add nothing to it. It must, rather, be done for its own sake, beyond argumentation. It is a matter of indifference how much rhetoric one employs to call it forth as an empirical event.

Index